MW01170750

Paleo Slow Cooker

Over 50 Quick and Easy Paleo Slow Cooker Recipes

Andrew Westbrook

Golden Road Publishing

Table of Contents

Soups, Stews, and Chowders 55

Fish and Seafood 75

Meat 92

Conclusion 111

Introduction

So, you want to get started on the Paleo diet? Very nice decision! This book is here to help you get acquainted with the diet and to aid you as you venture forth in a possibly life changing experience.

Like all diets, the Paleo diet will not be a simple one to follow at first, but after you understand some of the ins and outs of the diet, it will become second-nature to you. It's not one of the phony "cure-all" diets you see on television or in magazine ads. It's hard to compare the Paleo diet with other diets out there simply because of the fact that it's more of a lifestyle than a modern-day diet.

Nevertheless, this diet and lifestyle change is a tough undertaking and will require patience and plenty of self-discipline (trust me, you think that donut is tempting now, but it will be like the forbidden fruit once you start the Paleo diet). Everyone is capable of reaping the benefits of this lifestyle change if they put in the effort.

If you think you're ready, go ahead and turn the page and, please, enjoy the introduction to the Paleo diet.

Chapter 1: What Exactly is the Paleo Diet?

In short, the entire purpose of the Paleo diet is to revert our eating habits back to our ancestors' -- in that, you'll focus your eating habits around what the cavemen ate. Now, that doesn't mean you have to invent the time machine and hunt mammoths! It simply means that a lot of the foods we eat today -- foods that were not available to our cavemen ancestors -- are off the table (no pun intended).

A lot of your "typical" diets include something about not eating sugars or fats or processed foods. While all of these shouldn't be indulged in every day, it's not as simple as cutting the fat off your steak for dinner. However, anything processed is definitely off limits (which means most frozen foods, anything packed with preservatives, anything that requires a lot of processing to create, and of course all those sugary sweets).

So, what does that leave you to eat, aspiring paleo dieters? Well, think back to the days of hunting and gathering. If you keep that in mind, you'll have an easy little cheat sheet to help you remember what you can eat while abiding by the Paleo lifestyle: Anything that our ancestors could have hunted or gathered.

Chapter 2: The Hunting Grounds

One of the best, and easiest, ways to get protein in your body is through eating meat. Protein is essentially for muscle building as well as for repairing your tissue, growing hair and fingernails, and keeping your bones from getting too brittle. Protein, essentially, keeps your body as the armored tank of muscle and bones that it is. Without it, you'll be frailer.

There are other ways to obtain protein, of course. So don't worry, vegetarians! We'll get into that after we talk about the meats.

What meats can you eat while abiding by the rules of the Paleo diet? Simple: Any meats you eat now, you can eat while on the Paleo diet. Beef, pork, chicken and other birds, venison, etc. The list goes on. If you can buy it fresh at the grocery store or butcher's, or hunt it yourself, it's allowed in the Paleo diet.

It's worth pointing out that, yes, you should buy meat as fresh as you can. Whether you buy it from the butcher and have it wrapped up there, or even go to a farm yourself and buy half a cow to freeze yourself, fresh meat will, for the most part, be better for you.

What makes frozen or prepacked meats so unhealthy? Let's start with prepacked: It's not the worst way to buy meat, but it was packaged before it got to the store and usually has a longer shelf life.

Important food hunting fact: With most foods (there are some exceptions, of course), the longer the shelf life, the more preservatives are typically found in the food. While you should avoid eating large quantities of preservative-packed foods in your day-to-day life, you should especially avoid it while abiding by the Paleo diet. This is incredibly true for meats.

Frozen meats with long shelf lives (frozen chicken nuggets, breasts, tenders, or wings, for example) are packed with preservatives to make them easier to ship, stock, store, and serve. With the ease of the food comes a lot of harmful chemicals in those preservatives. Avoid them at all costs.

If you're not a fan of the red or white meats, seafood is always a valid option as well. While seafood may not have as high of levels of protein as a nice big steak, it does have less saturated fats, which always make for a lighter meal and, well, less fat. Seafood follows the same basic guidelines as meat: Buy fresh and watch out for those frozen and preservative-packed fish fillets that have long shelf lives.

There's a long list of seafood you can eat from fish (both freshwater and saltwater) to crustaceans, such as crabs, lobsters, and shrimp. The more options of food, the more variety and the more creative you can be.

Important food hunting fact: If you live in a landlocked country or state (somewhere like Missouri in the United States), don't fret. Explore your town and look for places that get fresh fish delivered to them directly. Sure, the fish might be a tad bit more expensive, but you'll notice a difference in quality and taste.

Meats have varying amounts of different proteins and other nutrients that you could, and probably should, take into account while planning meals when abiding by the Paleo diet. Below is a short and very basic guide to different meats and what they contain in the way of nutrients.

Meat 1: Beef

When you think meat, think protein-packed fuel for muscles. Beef can be divided into two subcategories: steak and ground beef (for hamburgers).

Steak has the highest amount of protein out of the meat departments, containing nearly double the amount of that found in chicken breasts and four times the amount found in most types of fish. While steak is a great source of protein, it does come at a cost: calories and fat content.

While fat is not terrible in small portions, and it adds so much to taste and texture, it is something that should be considered a treat and not a normal part of the menu.

Hamburger beef is a leaner solution to steak without giving up beef entirely. A (90% lean) patty consists of roughly the same amount of protein as a chicken breast (21 ½ grams) and much fewer calories and less fat than its steak counterpart.

Meat 2: Chicken

Like beef, chicken comes in two different subcategories, although this time the categories are divided by the type of meats found in a single chicken: white meat and dark meat.

White meat, which is much more common in KFC and chicken patties from take-out restaurants (not that you should go and eat from them), is a nice middle ground between steak and a lean hamburger patty. With nearly 30 grams of protein and 8 grams of fat, white chicken breasts are a relatively good source of protein and they contain little fat.

Dark chicken meat has similar protein to its lighter counterpart (around 26 grams per serving), but it has double the fat content at almost 16 grams of fat. While many people prefer the taste of dark meat chicken, white meat is more common and is a leaner cut of chicken.

Meat 3: Seafood

There are tons of fish in the sea, but for the sake of time, we're going to look at only one. It should be noted that the fish you are able to obtain in your town or city depends greatly on where your home is.

The first fish to look at is cod. Cod, like most fish, contains a decent amount of protein at about 23 grams. The protein levels are a bit lower than chicken or a beef patty, but not too far below to make a huge difference. The biggest difference between fish and the land-dwelling animals, however, is the amount of fat. While white meat chicken breast contains 8 grams of fat (a nice lean meat relatively), cod contains a mere nine-tenths of a gram of fat. That's right, 0.90 grams.

Fish is the perfect source of protein with as little fat as possible. Don't eat too much, though, because there is mercury in fish. Don't worry, fish fans, you'd have to eat a lot, *a lot* of fish before it starts to affect you.

Lobster, known as the "bougiest" of foods, is no longer for the rich and famous. While lobster can be daunting to cook and prepare, it's another fine source of protein, containing about 30 grams per cup of lobster. Similar to fish, lobster has a small amount of fat that goes along with that muscle-building protein (around 1.5 grams of fat per cup of lobster meat). Lobster is similar to fish in many nutritional ways.

Now, say you're not feeling either the grass-fed or water-dwelling sources of protein, but you still want to add a bit to your meal. Don't worry, there are tons of alternatives, primarily the nuts and seeds that you may gather from your local grocery store.

Chapter 3: Gathering Protein

Not all proteins come from those heavy and, potentially, fatty meats. An often overlooked source of protein comes in the forms of nuts and seeds. Nuts and seeds can easily provide you with a quick protein fix while going about your day, and they can be added to dishes to offer a unique flavor combination and, in some cases, a much needed crunch.

While, yes, the nuts and seeds aren't technically a food your caveman ancestors would hunt, they make for easy to store, easy to keep sources of protein that may mix up your meal plans.

Like meats, not all nuts and seeds share the same amount of protein and other nutrients you need to stay as healthy as possible while sticking to your new diet and lifestyle. Below is a brief description of some of the different kinds of nuts and seeds to help start you with your gathering of proteins.

Source 1: Soybeans

Soy has become a popular source of protein for vegetarians and omnivores alike over the last couple of decades. While it may not be the best source of protein on the market, these small treats definitely don't shy away from the protein contest.

In a small bag of soybeans (around 100 grams), you'll find roughly 35 grams of protein, placing it higher on the list than several meats listed in the previous chapter. Like those meats with a higher protein amount, the amount of fat in soybeans is also higher than many other sources (coming in at around 25.5 grams per that same 100 grams of soybeans).

Soybeans are a perfect contender against any meat for the protein and fat content.

Source 2: Peanuts

One of the most recognizable foods out there, the peanut also offers a bit of protein for those looking to add a bit of protein throughout their day. An ounce of peanuts can contain up to 7 grams of protein (which is not bad for the amount) and about 14 grams of fat.

While peanuts are not a food you would want to snack on all day and every day, they do make a great snack to eat by the handful every now and again (or a supplement to a protein-light meal to make sure you're getting all your valuable nutrients).

Source 3: Brown Rice

A grain people don't often consider as a source of protein is rice; specifically, brown rice. Roughly one-half of a cup of brown rice (one serving for those keeping track) has two and a half grams of protein. It doesn't seem like a lot, and relative to meats and nuts and seeds, it's not. But if you consider mixing chicken or nuts into your rice for a nice Chinese-inspired meal, then you're talking extra protein for those muscles.

While brown rice doesn't offer a ton of protein per serving, it also contains very little fat (about 1 gram per serving to be exact). So, yes, rice isn't enough on its own to give you a full dose of protein or fat, but it works well with other foods to provide that extra bit you may need for your day.

Those are only some examples of different sources of protein that will help you get the amount of the nutrients you need while staying faithful to your Paleo lifestyle. The most fun, however, comes from finding new and exotic sources to implement in your cooking to make it your own. And, of course, this is all without even looking into vegetables and fruits.

Chapter 4: Gathering Plants

The second part of our ancestors' lifestyle, which was mentioned in the previous chapter, is gathering. And yes, while gathering proteins from nuts, beans, seeds, and some grains (like brown rice) is important, finding fruits and vegetables is essential if you want to stay balanced and at the peak of health.

While it's true that certain fruits and vegetables contain small amounts of protein, it's probably safest to not assume them to be a good source of the stuff (unless, of course, you want to eat 110 apples to get the same amount of protein as you can find in a steak). This is why we look to plants to fulfill the other needs our bodies have.

Fruits and vegetables contain assortments of different vitamins, minerals, and that little bit of protein. One aspect of fruits that people often overlook is sugar, which is arguably one of the most important parts of fruits.

Why are sugars within fruits so important? Well, often times, when we experience fatigue throughout the day or even a craving for something sweet, it's our bodies telling us that we need sugar in our blood. While a donut can make your mouth water at the mere mention of it, apples actually contain more sugar, and will help your body feel revitalized quicker.

What does that say about eating habits? Simply put, when you feel tired or fatigued all day, don't go for the coffee or, worst of all, the sugary sweets right away. Consider the apple in all its glory and get some natural sugar into your body, not the preserved or caffeinated treats that are all too common.

Chapter 5: Parting Remarks

Now you know some of the basics of the Paleo diet and the foods that our ancestors ate to stay as healthy as they were. It's now up to you to decide if you want to move forward with this exciting new lifestyle, or try another option. This diet may not be for every single person out there, but remember all diets take work and self-discipline, so be prepared to struggle through temptation and be healthier for it.

Let's now get into the recipes!

Good luck!

Breakfast

Sausage, Egg, Bell Pepper, and Spinach Frittata

Prep Time: 15 minutes; **Cook Time:** 2-3 hours on LOW	

Serving Size: 124 g; **Serves**: 6; **Calories**: 201	
Total Fat: 14.6 g **Saturated Fat**: 4.6 g; **Trans Fat**: 0 g	
Protein: 13.8 g; **Total Carbs:** 3.4 g	
Dietary Fiber: 0.6 g**; Sugars**: 2.2 g	
Cholesterol: 244 mg; **Sodium**: 628 mg; **Potassium**: 255 mg	
Vitamin A: 33%; **Vitamin C**: 99%; **Calcium**: 4%; **Iron**: 10%	
Good points: High in selenium, high in vitamin A, and very high in vitamin C.	

Ingredients:
- 8 eggs, beaten
- 3/4 cups frozen spinach, drained
- 1/4 cups red onion, diced
- 1/2 teaspoons black pepper
- 1 teaspoon sea salt
- 1 1/3 cups breakfast sausage, cooked
- 1 1/2 cups red bell pepper, diced

Directions:
1. Generously grease the slow cooker. Put the sausage, spinach, red onions, red pepper, eggs, sea salt, and black pepper in the cooker and toss to combine.
2. Close the lid of the cooker and cook for 2-3 hours on LOW or until the frittata is well set.

Notes: If making ahead of time, let cool slightly and cut into equal-sized square portions. Store in individual freezable bags and freeze. When ready to serve, reheat for about 30-60 seconds in the microwave or until warmed.

Breakfast Meatloaf

Prep Time: 10 minutes; **Cook Time:** 3 hours on LOW	

Prep Time: 10 minutes; **Cook Time:** 3 hours on LOW

Serving Size: 294 g; **Serves**: 4; **Calories:** 443

Total Fat: 17 g **Saturated Fat**: 6. g; **Trans Fat**: 0.1 g

Protein: 64.2 g; **Total Carbs:** 6.6 g

Dietary Fiber: 2.6 g; **Sugars:** 1.9 g

Cholesterol: 247 mg; **Sodium:** 1099 mg; **Potassium:** 1141 mg

Vitamin A: 26%; **Vitamin C**: 8%; **Calcium:** 7%; **Iron**: 23%

Good points: Low in sugar, high in niacin, high in phosphorus, high in riboflavin, very high in selenium, very high in thiamin, and very high in vitamin B6.

Ingredients:

- 2 pounds ground pork
- 2 eggs
- 1/4 cup almond flour
- 1 teaspoon marjoram
- 1 teaspoon dried oregano
- 1 teaspoon crushed red pepper flake
- 1 tablespoon smoked paprika
- 1 tablespoon fresh sage, minced
- 1 tablespoon coconut oil
- 1 onion, diced
- 2 teaspoons sea salt
- 3 garlic cloves, minced

Directions:

1. Put the coconut oil in a skillet and heat over medium-high heat. Add the onion and sauté until soft. Add the garlic and sauté for about 3-4 minutes or until fragrant. Remove from the heat and then set aside. Let cool slightly.

2. Put the pork in a mixing bowl. Add the rest of the ingredients and the sautéed garlic and onion. With clean hands, blend the mixture until evenly mixed – do not overmix or the meatloaf will become tough while it cooks.
3. Transfer the pork mixture into the slow cooker and shape it into a loaf shape – ensure that the meatloaf does not touch any side of the slow cooker.
4. Close the lid of the cooker and cook for 3 hours on LOW. When cooked, immediately remove the meatloaf from the cooker. Otherwise, the meatloaf will become dry.
5. Let the meatloaf slightly cool and then cut into slices. Transfer the meatloaf into an airtight container.
6. In the morning, add a small amount of oil into a skillet on medium-high heat. Put a slice of meatloaf in the skillet and cook until both sides are browned. Serve immediately.

Notes: If you make this on the afternoon of a Sunday, then you will have a quick breakfast every morning for 1 week.

Pumpkin Pie Sorghum Breakfast

Prep Time: 10 minutes; **Cook Time:** 8 hours on LOW	
Serving Size: 203 g; **Serves**: 4; **Calories:** 299	
Total Fat: 1.2 g **Saturated Fat**: 0 g; **Trans Fat**: 0 g	
Protein: 0.8 g; **Total Carbs:** 73.8 g	
Dietary Fiber: 1.8 g; **Sugars:** 69.5 g	
Cholesterol: 0 mg; **Sodium**: 56 mg; **Potassium**: 998 mg	
Vitamin A: 143%; **Vitamin C**: 4%; **Calcium**: 23%; **Iron**: 24%	
Good points: Very low in saturated fat, no cholesterol, low in sodium, very high in manganese, and very high in vitamin A.	

Ingredients:
- 1 cup sorghum, rinsed (I used Bob's Red Mill Gluten-Free Whole-Grain Sorghum)
- 1 cup unsweetened almond milk
- 1 tablespoon pumpkin pie spice (I used Simply Organic Pumpkin Pie Spice)
- 1 teaspoon pure vanilla extract
- 2 tablespoons pure maple syrup
- 3/4 cup pumpkin purée (not pumpkin pie filling)

Directions:
1. Put all of the ingredients in a 3-4 quarts slow cooker. Pour in 2 cups of water and combine, stirring well until mixed.
2. Close the lid of the cooker and cook for 8 hours on LOW or until the liquid is absorbed or the sorghum is tender.

Notes: You can store this dish in individual servings on a covered container. When ready to serve, just scoop it out, put in a small-sized saucepan, add a splash of water or almond milk, and cook on medium heat or until heated through.

Ham and Spinach Frittata

Prep Time: 5 minutes; **Cook Time:** 1 hour, 30 min	

Prep Time: 5 minutes; **Cook Time:** 1 hour, 30 min

Serving Size: 82 g; **Serves**: 8; **Calories:** 109

Total Fat: 6.9 g **Saturated Fat**: 2.2 g; **Trans Fat**: 0 g

Protein: 9.9 g; **Total Carbs:** 1.8 g

Dietary Fiber: 0 g; **Sugars:** 0.8 g

Cholesterol: 214 mg; **Sodium**: 300 mg; **Potassium**: 157 mg

Vitamin A: 17%; **Vitamin C**: 27%; **Calcium**: 4%; **Iron**: 7%

Good points: Gluten-free, low in sugar, high in phosphorus, high in riboflavin, very high in selenium, high in vitamin A, high in vitamin B12, and very high in vitamin C.

Ingredients:
- 10 eggs, large-sized
- 1/2 green bell pepper, diced
- 1 cup ham, diced
- 2 handfuls fresh spinach
- Salt and pepper

Equipment:
- 1 slow cooker liner

Directions:
1. Line a 6-quart, oval-shaped slow cooker with the liner and grease with nonstick cooking spray.
2. Put the ham, spinach, and peppers into the slow cooker.
3. Crack the eggs into a bowl. Add the pepper, salt, and whisk until completely scrambled. Pour the beaten eggs into the slow cooker.
4. Close the lid of the cooker and cook for 1 1/2-2 hours on HIGH or until the center of the

frittata no longer jiggles when you shake the slow cooker.

5. Lift out the slow cooker pot and slide out the liner with a spatula. Slice the frittata into squares and serve.

Notes: You can also cook this in a 4-quart slow cooker – just reduce the ingredients to 1/2 their original amount.

Paleo Sausage, Kale, Leek, Egg, and Sweet Potato Breakfast Casserole

Prep Time: 15 minutes; **Cook Time:** 6 hours on LOW	

Prep Time: 15 minutes; **Cook Time:** 6 hours on LOW

Serving Size: 152 g; **Serves**: 6; **Calories:** 299

Total Fat: 23 g **Saturated Fat**: 10.2 g; **Trans Fat**: 0 g

Protein: 13.3 g; **Total Carbs:** 10.3 g

Dietary Fiber: 1.3 g; **Sugars:** 2.7 g

Cholesterol: 243 mg; **Sodium:** 377 mg; **Potassium**: 344 mg

Vitamin A: 48%; **Vitamin C**: 39%; **Calcium**: 6%; **Iron**: 16%

Good Points: Low in sugar, high in selenium, high in vitamin A, very high in vitamin B6, and high in vitamin C.

Ingredients:
- 1 1/2 cups beef sausage, preferably homemade
- 1 1/3 cups leek, sliced
- 1 cup kale, chopped
- 2 tablespoons coconut oil
- 2 teaspoons garlic, minced
- 2/3 cups sweet potato, peeled and grated
- 8 eggs

Directions:
1. Put the coconut oil in a skillet and melt over medium heat. Add the leeks, kale, garlic, and sauté until the kale is just wilted.
2. In a large-sized bowl, add the eggs and beat. Add the beef sausage, sweet potato, and sautéed vegetables, and stir to combine.
3. Pour the egg mixture into the slow cooker. Close the lid of the cooker and cook for 6 hours on LOW.

Notes: If making ahead of time, let completely cool. Cut the casserole into equal sizes, store in individual freezer bags, label, and freeze. When ready to serve, just reheat for 1-2 minutes in a microwave or until warmed through.

Paleo Mexican-Style Breakfast Casserole

Prep Time: 15 minutes; **Cook Time:** 6-8 hours on LOW	

Prep Time: 15 minutes; **Cook Time:** 6-8 hours on LOW

Serving Size: 200 g; **Serves**: 6; **Calories:** 213

Total Fat: 10 g **Saturated Fat**: 3.1 g; **Trans Fat**: 0 g

Protein: 22.2 g; **Total Carbs:** 7.1 g

Dietary Fiber: 1 g; **Sugars:** 2.9 g

Cholesterol: 260 mg; **Sodium**: 458 mg; **Potassium**: 345 mg

Vitamin A: 20%; **Vitamin C**: 68%; **Calcium**: 8%; **Iron**: 14%

Good points: Very high in phosphorus, high in riboflavin, very high in selenium, very high in vitamin B6, and very high in vitamin C.

Ingredients:
- 1 package (8 ounce) mushrooms, chopped, optional
- 1 red bell pepper, chopped
- 1 sweet potato, shredded or cubed
- 1 yellow onion, chopped
- 1/2 packet taco seasoning OR make you are own for a strict paleo
- 1/2 pound turkey bacon
- 8 eggs, whisked
- Salsa, guacamole, and jalapeno, to garnish

Directions:
1. In a skillet, fry the turkey bacon until crispy. Transfer into a plate and set aside. When cool enough to touch, crumble.
2. In the same skillet, cook the onions until soft. Transfer into the slow cooker. Add the crumbled bacon, sweet potato, bell pepper, eggs, and mushrooms in the cooker, and stir to combine.

3. Sprinkle the taco seasoning over the ingredients in the cooker and stir to dissolve.
4. Close the lid of the cooker and cook for 6-8 hours on LOW. Slice and serve with salsa, guacamole, and jalapeno.

Creamy Avocado and Egg Breakfast

Prep Time: 5 minutes; **Cook Time:** 45 minutes on HIGH	
Serving Size: 145 g; **Serves:** 2; **Calories:** 268	
Total Fat: 24 g **Saturated Fat**: 5.5 g; **Trans Fat**: 0 g	
Protein: 7.5 g; **Total Carbs:** 9 g	
Dietary Fiber: 6.7 g; **Sugars:** 0.8 g	
Cholesterol: 164 mg; **Sodium**: 68 mg; **Potassium**: 547 mg	
Vitamin A: 7%; **Vitamin C**: 17%; **Calcium**: 4%; **Iron**: 8%	
Good points: Low in sodium and low in sugar.	

Ingredients:

- 2 eggs
- 1 avocado, large-sized
- Cracked black pepper

Directions:

1. Set the slow cooker to HIGH. Lay a sheet of baking paper in the bottom of the cooker.
2. Cut the avocado into half and remove the seed. With the cut side facing up, put the avocado in the baking paper. Carefully crack 1 egg into the seed-hollowed part of each avocado half. Sprinkle with black pepper to taste.
3. Close the lid of the cooker and cook for 45 minutes on HIGH or until the eggs are cooked to your liking.

Overnight Paleo "Pear Oatmeal"

Prep Time: 15 minutes; **Cook Time:** 7-8 hours on LOW	
Serving Size: 523 g; **Serves:** 4-6; **Calories:** 783	
Total Fat: 60.5 g **Saturated Fat:** 53.1 g; **Trans Fat:** 0 g	
Protein: 6.4 g; **Total Carbs:** 65.2 g	
Dietary Fiber: 18.3 g; **Sugars:** 39.4 g	
Cholesterol: 0 mg; **Sodium:** 37 mg; **Potassium:** 949 mg	
Vitamin A: 2%; **Vitamin C:** 35%; **Calcium:** 5%; **Iron:** 63%	
Good points: No cholesterol and very low in sodium.	

Ingredients:

- 6 pears, ripe-fruit, seeds removed and then chopped, skin on or removed
- 3 cups coconut, finely shredded
- 2/3 cup coconut butter
- 2 tablespoons coconut oil OR ghee, grass-fed
- 1/2 teaspoon ground cinnamon, preferably organic
- 1 tablespoon organic vanilla extract (omit for AIP and whole 30)
- 1 can coconut milk, full fat, preferably organic and BPA free
- Sprinkle sea salt

Directions:

1. Set the slow cooker to LOW heat.
2. Put all of the ingredients into the slow cooker and stir to combine.
3. Close the lid of the cooker and cook for 7-8 hours on LOW or overnight. Enjoy!

Breakfast Paleo Chorizo Burrito

Prep Time: 10 minutes; **Cook Time:** 6-8 hours on LOW

Serving Size: 129 g; **Serves:** 10; **Calories:** 293

Total Fat: 22.7 g **Saturated Fat:** 8.2 g; **Trans Fat:** 0 g

Protein: 18.1 g; **Total Carbs:** 3.7 g

Dietary Fiber: 0.6 g; **Sugars:** 1.5 g

Cholesterol: 236 mg; **Sodium:** 791 mg; **Potassium:** 345 mg

Vitamin A: 7%; **Vitamin C:** 2%; **Calcium:** 4%; **Iron:** 11%

Good points: Low in sugar and high in selenium.

Ingredients:
- 12 eggs, preferably organic
- 1/4 cup cilantro
- 1 pound chorizo, crumbled
- 1 cup fresh salsa
- 1/2 small yellow onion, finely chopped
- 1 teaspoon onion powder
- 1 teaspoon garlic powder
- 1 teaspoon cumin
- Franks red hots
- Paleo tortilla
- Salt and freshly ground pepper, to taste

Directions:
1. Except for the salsa and eggs, put the rest of the ingredients into the slow cooker.
2. Crack the eggs into a bowl. Add the salsa and beat until whisked. Pour the egg mix over the ingredients in the cooker.
3. Close the lid of the cooker and cook for 6-8 hours on LOW.

4. When cooked, plate the egg-chorizo mixture over a large-sized paleo tortilla. Garnish with cilantro and serve.

Overnight Breakfast Casserole

Prep Time: 5-10 minutes; **Cook Time:** 6-8 hours on LOW

Serving Size: 224 g; **Serves**: 6-8; **Calories:** 447

Total Fat: 32.9 g **Saturated Fat**: 11.8 g; **Trans Fat**: 0 g

Protein: 28.3 g; **Total Carbs:** 9.6 g

Dietary Fiber: 2.3 g; **Sugars:** 3.8 g

Cholesterol: 391 mg; **Sodium**: 895 mg; **Potassium**: 598 mg

Vitamin A: 24%; **Vitamin C**: 77%; **Calcium**: 7%; **Iron**: 24%

Good points: Low in sugar, high in selenium, very high in vitamin B6, and high in vitamin C.

Ingredients:
- 1 pound breakfast sausage, sugar-free
- 1 red pepper, diced
- 1 sweet potato, large-sized, grated or shredded
- 1 teaspoon dried basil
- 1 teaspoon dried oregano
- 1 teaspoon garlic powder
- 1/2 teaspoon salt PLUS to taste
- 1/2 yellow or sweet onion, diced
- 1/4 cup coconut milk, full-fat
- 1/4 teaspoon black pepper
- 12 eggs, whisked
- 2 tablespoons nutritional yeast

Directions:
1. Whisk the eggs, dice all the vegetables, and shred/grate the sweet potato with a hand grater or with the shredding attachment of a food processor.
2. Lightly grease the slow cooker with the coconut oil. Put all of the ingredients in the cooker. Crumble the meat as you toss the ingredients to

break it up into small chunks. Use a large-sized spoon to combine the ingredients well.
3. Close the lid of the cooker and cook for 6-8 hours on LOW. When cooked, slice and serve.

Breakfast Chicken Soup

Prep Time: 10 minutes; **Cook Time:** 10 hours	
Serving Size: 716 g; **Serves**: 6; **Calories:** 609	
Total Fat: 25.7 g **Saturated Fat**: 6.9 g; **Trans Fat**: 0 g	
Protein: 87.9 g; **Total Carbs:** 1.6 g	
Dietary Fiber: 1.2 g; **Sugars:** 0 g	
Cholesterol: 269 mg; **Sodium**: 312 mg; **Potassium**: 827 mg	
Vitamin A: 5%; **Vitamin C**: 4%; **Calcium**: 6%; **Iron**: 21%	
Good points: Low in sodium, very low in sugar, very high in niacin, high in selenium, and high in vitamin B6.	

Ingredients:
- 1 whole chicken
- 2 1/2 quarts water OR chicken stock OR bone broth
- Fine sea salt, to taste

For each serving of soup:
- 1/2 avocado, chopped
- 2 tablespoons fresh cilantro OR Italian parsley, chopped
- 2 tablespoons scallions, chopped

Directions:
1. Put the chicken into a 6-quart slow cooker. Pour the liquids over the chicken – use chicken broth for extra flavor.
2. Close the lid of the cooker and cook for 10 hours on LOW or until the meat falls off the bones. Take the chicken out from the cooker and separate the meat from the bones.
3. Using a fork, pull the chicken meat apart – save the bones to make more bone broth for another day. Season the broth with salt to taste.

4. For each serving, add 2 tablespoons of scallions, 2 tablespoons of fresh herbs, and 1/2 of an avocado. Enjoy!

Lunch

Chicken Fajitas

Prep Time: 15 minutes; **Cook Time:** 6-8 hours on LOW; 3-4 hours on HIGH

Serving Size: 206 g; **Serves**: 6; **Calories:** 248	
Total Fat: 8.8 g **Saturated Fat**: 2.4 g; **Trans Fat**: 0 g	
Protein: 33.9 g; **Total Carbs:** 7.3 g	
Dietary Fiber: 1.4 g; **Sugars:** 2.8 g	
Cholesterol: 101 mg; **Sodium:** 604 mg; **Potassium:** 432 mg	
Vitamin A: 14%; **Vitamin C**: 29%; **Calcium:** 5%; **Iron**: 12%	
Good points: Very high in niacin, high in selenium, high in vitamin B6, and high in vitamin C.	

Ingredients:
- 1 can (14.5 ounces) petite diced tomatoes with green chilies
- 1 orange, red, and green bell pepper, sliced
- 2 pounds chicken breast halves, boneless skinless
- 2 1/2 teaspoon chili powder
- 1 yellow onion, large-sized, halved and then sliced
- 1 teaspoon salt
- 1 teaspoon paprika
- 2 teaspoons ground cumin
- 3/4 teaspoon ground coriander
- 3/4 teaspoon pepper
- 4 cloves garlic, minced

Directions:
1. In a bowl, combine the pepper, salt, coriander, cumin, and chili powder until well mixed.

39

2. Pour the canned tomatoes into the slow cooker. Add 1/2 of the red and green bell peppers and 1/2 of the onion. Top with the minced garlic.
3. Dip the chicken breasts into the seasoning mix, covering both sides of the chicken. Add into the slow cooker, placing them on top of the peppers. Add the remaining 1/2 of the peppers and onion on top of the chicken breasts.
4. Close the lid of the cooker and cook for 6-8 hours on LOW or for 3-4 hours on HIGH.
5. When cooked, shred the chicken breasts. Top with toppings like cheese, sour cream, and pico.

Carnitas and Paleo Nachos

Prep Time: 15 minutes; **Cook Time:** 8-12 hours on LOW	

Serving Size: 506 g; **Serves:** 6-8; **Calories:** 853

Total Fat: 57.4 g **Saturated Fat:** 20.9 g; **Trans Fat:** 0 g

Protein: 64.2 g; **Total Carbs:** 18.9 g

Dietary Fiber: 3.6 g; **Sugars:** 12.1 g

Cholesterol: 238 mg; **Sodium:** 314 mg; **Potassium:** 1329 mg

Vitamin A: 159%; **Vitamin C:** 771%; **Calcium:** 10%; **Iron:** 31%

Good points: Low in sodium, high in selenium, high in thiamin, high in vitamin A, and very high in vitamin C.

Ingredients:
For the carnitas:
- 3 1/2 pounds pork shoulder
- 1 cup chicken stock or broth
- 1 1/2 tablespoons fresh thyme leaves
- 4 bay leaves
- Olive oil
- Sea salt and pepper, to taste, be generous

For the paleo nachos:
- Small sweet peppers, halved
- Carnitas, recipe above

Choice of toppings:
- Avocado, chopped
- Cilantro, chopped
- Red onion, chopped
- Jalapeños, chopped
- Salsa verde

Directions:
For the carnitas:

1. Generously rub the pork shoulder with the pepper and salt.
2. Put the oil in a skillet and heat on high heat. Put the pork shoulder in the skillet and cook each side for 3-4 minutes or until browned to seal the juices in the meat.
3. Pour the broth in the slow cooker – the broth is not meant to cover the pork to maintain the crispy exterior just like real carnitas that you eat in Mexico. Add the pork, thyme, and bay leaves.
4. Close the lid of the cooker and cook for 8-12 hours on LOW. When the pork is cooked, shred and enjoy!
5. When reheating, fry the meat in the stove top to crisp it.

For the paleo nachos:
1. Fill the peppers with the pork meat and broil in the oven for about 5 to 6 minutes or until the edges are slightly browned and the top of the carnitas are crisp – do not cook them for too long or the peppers will become too soft and difficult to eat with your hands. Top with your favorite toppings. Enjoy!

Notes: Serve on top of cilantro-cauliflower rice with lettuce, salsa, etc.

Slow Cooked Paleo Chicken Salad

Prep Time: 10 minutes; **Cook Time:** 90 minutes on HIGH, 4 hours on LOW

Serving Size: 303 g; **Serves**: 2; **Calories:** 543	

Serving Size: 303 g; **Serves**: 2; **Calories:** 543

Total Fat: 35 g **Saturated Fat**: 9 g; **Trans Fat**: 0 g

Protein: 36.2 g; **Total Carbs:** 24.3 g

Dietary Fiber: 8 g; **Sugars:** 13.8 g

Cholesterol: 101 mg; **Sodium**: 937 mg; **Potassium**: 937 mg

Vitamin A: 13%; **Vitamin C**: 31%; **Calcium**: 6%; **Iron**: 16%

Ingredients:
For the salad:
- 100 grams cherry tomatoes
- 1 avocado, small-sized
- 25 grams mixed lettuce

For the salad dressing:
- 1 teaspoon white wine vinaigrette
- 1 teaspoon olive oil
- 1 teaspoon mustard
- 1 teaspoon honey
- Salt and pepper

For the slow cooked chicken:
- 2 pieces chicken breasts
- 1 teaspoon mustard
- 1 teaspoon garlic puree
- 1 teaspoon coconut oil
- 1 teaspoon chives
- 1 tablespoon honey
- Salt and pepper

Directions:

1. In a mixing bowl, put the honey, coconut oil, garlic, seasoning, and mix well to make a sticky marinade. Put the chicken on a chopping board and season with pepper and salt.
2. Put the chicken into a sheet of silver foil. Add the honey mixture. Toss the chicken a few times to coat. Seal the foil well and put in the slow cooker.
3. Close the lid of the cooker and cook for 90 minutes on HIGH. When the chicken is cooked, set aside.
4. In a salad dish, mix all of the ingredients into the salad dish that you are planning to eat. Put the lettuce on top and then follow with the avocado slices.
5. Chop the cherry tomatoes into halves and season with pepper and salt. Add them to the salad.
6. Chop the cooked chicken into chunks and add into the salad. Serve!

Notes: If you have more time, you can cook the chicken for 4 hours on LOW.

Chicken Tacos

Prep Time: 5 minutes; **Cook Time:** 6-8 hours on LOW

Serving Size: 184 g; **Serves**: 4-6; **Calories:** 228

Total Fat: 8.5 g **Saturated Fat**: 2.3 g; **Trans Fat**: 0 g

Protein: 33.4 g; **Total Carbs:** 2.8 g

Dietary Fiber: 0.8 g; **Sugars:** 1.9 g

Cholesterol: 101 mg; **Sodium**: 101 mg; **Potassium**: 444 mg

Vitamin A: 13%; **Vitamin C**: 16%; **Calcium**: 2%; **Iron**: 9%

Good points: Low in sodium, low in sugar, very high in niacin, high in phosphorus, high in selenium, and high in vitamin B6.

Ingredients:
- 4 chicken breasts, boneless, skinless
- 1 can Rotel tomatoes
- Taco seasoning, to taste

Directions:
1. Put all of the ingredients into the slow cooker.
2. Close the lid of the cooker and cook for 6-8 hours on LOW.
3. When the chicken is cooked, shred and use in salad.
4. You can serve it hot or cold. It would be great as leftovers. You can take it as lunch as well.

Chicken Burritos

Prep Time: 5 minutes; **Cook Time:** 3-4 hours on HIGH	

Prep Time: 5 minutes; **Cook Time:** 3-4 hours on HIGH

Serving Size: 601 g; **Serves:** 4-6; **Calories:** 733

Total Fat: 27.5 g **Saturated Fat:** 7.3 g; **Trans Fat:** 0 g

Protein: 102.2 g; **Total Carbs:** 14 g

Dietary Fiber: 2.4 g; **Sugars:** 3 g

Cholesterol: 300 mg; **Sodium:** 1041 mg; **Potassium:** 1353 mg

Vitamin A: 55%; **Vitamin C:** 118%; **Calcium:** 63%; **Iron:** 15%

Good points: Low in sugar, very high in magnesium, high in niacin, very high in phosphorus, high in selenium, and high in vitamin C.

Ingredients:
- 4 boneless chicken breast
- 2 teaspoons ground cumin
- 2 tablespoons chili powder
- 2 cans Rotel tomatoes
- 1 tablespoon fajita seasoning
- 1 onion, chopped
- 1 bell pepper, chopped

Directions:
1. Put all of the ingredients into the slow cooker.
2. Close the lid of the cooker and cook for 3-4 hours on HIGH. When cooked, the chicken should be tender enough that they fall apart when stirring. Shred the chicken meat using 2 forks.
3. Return the shredded meat into the slow cooker and stir to combine and coat with the cooking juices.
4. Serve the shredded meat with shredded cheese. Add any of your desired toppings and roll into burritos.

Pulled Chicken

Prep Time: 5 minutes; **Cook Time:** 5-6 hours on HIGH; 8-10 hours on LOW

Serving Size: 491 g; **Serves**: 6-8; **Calories:** 700

Total Fat: 13.8 g **Saturated Fat**: 3.9 g; **Trans Fat**: 0 g

Protein: 131.9 g; **Total Carbs:** 3.5 g

Dietary Fiber: 0.8 g; **Sugars:** 1.6 g

Cholesterol: 349 mg; **Sodium:** 330 mg; **Potassium**: 903 mg

Vitamin A: 2%; **Vitamin C**: 4%; **Calcium**: 7%; **Iron**: 23%

Good points: Low in sodium, very low in sugar, very high in niacin, high in phosphorus, very high in selenium, and high in vitamin B6.

Ingredients:
- 1 piece (6-7 pounds) chicken
- 2 onions, small-sized, peeled, optional
- 3-4 tablespoons scratch seasoning, recipe below

For the chicken scratch seasoning:
- 1 tablespoon black pepper
- 1 tablespoon cayenne pepper
- 1 tablespoon dried thyme
- 1 tablespoon onion powder
- 1 tablespoon white pepper
- 3 tablespoons garlic powder
- 3 tablespoons paprika
- 3 tablespoons salt

Directions:
1. In a large-sized airtight container, mix all of the chicken scratch seasoning ingredients. You can use a large-sized used spice container that still has its top on for easy use.

47

2. Wash the chicken well and then pat dry using paper towels. Season the chicken all over with the mixture of scratch seasoning. If using onions, stuff them inside of the chicken. Put the chicken in the slow cooker – no need to add any water; the chicken will produce its own cooking liquid.
3. Close the lid of the slow cooker and cook for 5-6 hours on HIGH or for 8-10 hours on LOW.
4. After cooking time, turn off the slow cooker. Let the chicken rest for about 30-45 minutes with the slow cooker lid on.
5. Using whatever utensils needed - you can use tongs and a big slotted spoon – remove the chicken from the slow cooker. Reserve the broth for another use.
6. Remove the bones, skin, etc. from the chicken. Using 2 forks, shred or pull the meat into bite-sized pieces.
7. If desired, you can also as-is with BBQ sauce on the side.

Notes: Use any leftover to make quesadillas, chicken salad, chicken pot, or anything else you can think of.

You can generously season chicken or any poultry with the scratch seasoning since it is 25 percent less salt.

Pot Roast for French Dip Sandwiches

Prep Time: 5 minutes; **Cook Time:** 6-8 hours on HIGH

Serving Size: 253 g; **Serves:** 6; **Calories:** 440

Total Fat: 15.9 g **Saturated Fat:** 5.6 g; **Trans Fat:** 0 g

Protein: 68.8 g; **Total Carbs:** 0.7 g

Dietary Fiber: 0 g; **Sugars:** 0.5 g

Cholesterol: 207 mg; **Sodium:** 152 mg; **Potassium:** 917 mg

Vitamin A: 0%; **Vitamin C:** 0%; **Calcium:** 0%; **Iron:** 237%

Good points: Low in sodium, very low in sugar, very high in iron, high in niacin, high in phosphorus, very high in selenium, very high in vitamin B6, very high in vitamin B12, and very high in zinc.

Ingredients:
For the pot roast:
- 3-pound beef roast
- 2 packets Italian seasoning mix
- 1/2 cup water

For serving:
- French baguette, hoagie rolls, French rolls, or other Paleo-style bread
- Au jus, your favorite recipe

Directions:
1. Pour the water into the slow cooker. Add the pot roast in the cooker.
2. Sprinkle the roast with the Italian seasoning mix – make sure to cover the bottom and the sides.
3. Close the lid of the cooker and cook for 6-8 hours on HIGH.
4. After the cooking time is up, pull the meat apart using 2 forks. Return pulled meat into

the slow cooker to keep warm and absorb the remaining cooking juices.
5. Serve in Paleo bread and au jus on the side as dipping.

Paleo Sloppy Joe

Prep Time: 15 minutes; **Cook Time:** 2 hours on LOW

Serving Size: 329 g; **Serves:** 8; **Calories:** 647

Total Fat: 27.1 g **Saturated Fat**: 9 g; **Trans Fat**: 0 g

Protein: 55.5 g; **Total Carbs:** 42.8 g

Dietary Fiber: 2.5 g; **Sugars:** 21.1 g

Cholesterol: 148 mg; **Sodium**: 1835 mg; **Potassium**: 999 mg

Vitamin A: 17%; **Vitamin C**: 56%; **Calcium**: 9%; **Iron**: 135%

Good points: Very high in iron, high in selenium, very high in vitamin B6, and very high in vitamin B12.

Ingredients:
- 2 pounds ground beef
- 12 ounces bacon, hickory smoked, sliced into 1/2-inch pieces
- 1 yellow onion, diced
- 1 green bell pepper, diced
- Paleo BBQ sauce, recipe below
- Paleo buns, to serve

For the Paleo BBQ sauce:
- 15 ounces canned tomato sauce
- 2 tablespoons maple syrup
- 2 teaspoons mustard
- 3/4 cup water
- 3/4 teaspoon onion powder
- 1/4 cup balsamic vinegar
- 1/3 cup honey OR your vegan sweetener of choice, such as agave)
- 1 teaspoon smoked paprika
- 1 teaspoon real salt

Directions:

1. In a large-sized skillet, crumble and brown the ground beef. Transfer the browned beef into the slow cooker.
2. In the same skillet, add the diced bacon and cook until beginning to brown. Add the green peppers and onion into the skillet. Continue sautéing until the bacon is completely cooked and the pepper and onion are translucent and soft.
3. Add the bacon mixture into the slow cooker.
4. Add all of the BBQ sauce ingredients into the slow cooker and stir well to combine.
5. Close the lid of the cooker and cook for 2 hours on LOW.
6. Serve on your favorite Paleo hamburger buns.

Shredded Beef Sandwiches

Prep Time: 5 minutes; **Cook Time:** 10-12 hours on LOW

Serving Size: 130 g; **Serves:** 12; **Calories:** 216

Total Fat: 7.1 g **Saturated Fat**: 2.7 g; **Trans Fat**: 0 g

Protein: 34.5 g; **Total Carbs:** 1.1 g

Dietary Fiber: 0 g; **Sugars:** 0 g

Cholesterol: 101 mg; **Sodium**: 172 mg; **Potassium**: 477 mg

Vitamin A: 0%; **Vitamin C**: 1%; **Calcium**: 1%; **Iron**: 119%

Good points: Very low in sugar, very high in iron, high in niacin, high in phosphorus, very high in selenium, very high in vitamin B6, very high in vitamin B12, and very high in zinc.

Ingredients:
- 1 piece (3 pounds) beef roast, boneless
- 1 onion, medium-sized, chopped
- 1/2 teaspoon salt, optional
- 1/3 cup vinegar
- 1/4 teaspoon ground cloves
- 1/8 teaspoon garlic powder
- 3 bay leaves

Directions:
1. Cut the roast into halves and put in the slow cooker.
2. Add all the rest of the ingredients in the cooker.
3. Close the lid of the cooker and cook for 10-12 hours on LOW or until the meat is very tender.
4. When cooked, discard the bay leaves. Remove the meat from the cooker and shred using a fork.
5. Serve the shredded meat on Paleo buns.

Paleo Crock Pot Chicken Tacos

Prep Time: 5 minutes; **Cook Time:** 3 1/2-4 hours on LOW

Serving Size: 305 g; **Serves:** 4; **Calories:** 296

Total Fat: 5.4 g **Saturated Fat:** 1.5 g; **Trans Fat:** 0 g

Protein: 51.2 g; **Total Carbs:** 9.2 g

Dietary Fiber: 2.2 g; **Sugars:** 4.2 g

Cholesterol: 131 mg; **Sodium:** 788 mg; **Potassium:** 688 mg

Vitamin A: 8%; **Vitamin C:** 9%; **Calcium:** 6%; **Iron:** 12%

Ingredients:
- 1 1/2 pounds chicken breasts
- 1 jar (16 ounces) salsa
- 1/2 onion, diced
- 1/2 teaspoon cilantro
- 1/2 teaspoon oregano
- 1-2 limes, juiced
- 5-6 mini peppers, diced

Directions:
1. Dice the mini peppers and the onions. Put in the bottom of the slow cooker.
2. Put the chicken on top of the peppers and onions. Season with pepper, salt, oregano, and cilantro.
3. Pour the salsa over the chicken and top with the lime juice.
4. Close the lid of the cooker and cook for 3 1/2-4 hours on LOW.
5. Serve on lettuce taco with slices of avocados.

Soups, Stews, and Chowders

Split Pea and Ham Soup

Prep Time: 15 minutes; **Cook Time:** 8-10 hours LOW	
Serving Size: 419 g; **Serves**: 8; **Calories:** 394	
Total Fat: 10.4 g **Saturated Fat:** 3.4 g; **Trans Fat**: 0 g	
Protein: 33.1 g; **Total Carbs:** 42.3 g	
Dietary Fiber: 16.9 g; **Sugars:** 6.3 g	
Cholesterol: 65 mg; **Sodium**: 1804 mg; **Potassium**: 989 mg	
Vitamin A: 79%; **Vitamin C**: 13%; **Calcium**: 8%; **Iron**: 21%	
Good points: High in dietary fiber, high in manganese, high in selenium, high in thiamin, and high in vitamin A.	

Ingredients:
- 1 ham bone (2 pounds smoked pork hocks OR 2 pounds ham shanks
- 1 onion, medium-sized, chopped (about 1/2 cup)
- 1 package (16 ounces) dried split peas, sorted and rinsed (about 2 1/4 cups)
- 1 teaspoon salt
- 1/4 teaspoon pepper
- 2 stalks celery, medium-sized, finely chopped (1 cup)
- 3 carrots, medium-sized, cut into 1/4-inch slices (about 1 1/2 cups)
- 7 cups water

Directions:
1. Except for the ham, put the rest of the ingredients in a 4-5 quart slow cooker and stir to mix. Add the ham on top of the pea mixture.

2. Close the lid of the cooker and cook for 8-10 hours on LOW or until the peas are tender.
3. Remove the ham from the cooker and put on a cutting board. Pull the ham meat from the bones with 2 forks. Discard the skin and bones. Return the pulled ham meat into the soup. Stir well and serve.

Paleo Italian-Inspired Meatball Soup

Prep Time: 15 minutes; **Cook Time:** 8 hours on LOW; 5 hours on LOW	
Serving Size: 410 g; **Serves**: 6; **Calories:** 416	
Total Fat: 30.8 g **Saturated Fat**: 9.7 g; **Trans Fat**: 0 g	
Protein: 25.9 g; **Total Carbs:** 8.6 g	
Dietary Fiber: 2.4 g; **Sugars:** 4.6 g	
Cholesterol: 83 mg; **Sodium**: 1974 mg; **Potassium**: 850 mg	
Vitamin A: 15%; **Vitamin C**: 38%; **Calcium**: 4%; **Iron**: 13%	
Good points: High in niacin.	

Ingredients:
For the meatballs:
- 1 pound ground beef ground OR Italian sausage
- 1 /2 tablespoon Italian seasonings, organic
- 1 tablespoon coconut flour
- 1 tablespoon golden flax meal
- 1/2 teaspoon garlic powder
- 1/2 teaspoon sea salt
- 1/4 cup tomato sauce, organic OR home made

For the soup:
- 1 carrot, medium-sized, shredded or chopped, optional
- 1 jar (14 ounce) diced tomatoes, organic
- 1 teaspoon garlic powder
- 1 teaspoon sea salt
- 1 yellow squash medium-sized, chopped
- 1 zucchini, medium-sized, chopped
- 1/2 onion, medium-sized, minced, optional
- 1/4 cup pancetta OR 5 slices uncooked bacon, chopped (choose sugar-free and nitrate-free)
- 2 cloves garlic, minced

- 2 teaspoon Italian seasonings, organic
- 4 cups chicken broth, organic, gluten-free OR homemade

Directions:

1. In a large-sized mixing bowl, combine all of the meatball ingredients, kneading with your hands. Form 1 tablespoon of the meat mixture into balls using your hands. When the meatballs are formed, put a couple in a greased or oiled skillet over medium-high heat. Cook until all sides are browned – you do not need to cook them completely. Repeat the process until all the meatballs are browned.
2. Set the slow cooker to HIGH setting. Put the pancetta/bacon into the bottom of the cooker. Add the garlic. Put the browned meatballs on top of the garlic and the pancetta.
3. Close the lid of the cooker and cook for 8 hours on LOW or for 5 hours on LOW.
4. If you can have dairy, serve garnish with parmesan cheese.

Paleo Ham Parsnip Chowder

Prep Time: 10 minutes; **Cook Time:** 3 hours on LOW	
Serving Size: 329 g; **Serves**: 5; **Calories:** 424	
Total Fat: 17.1 g **Saturated Fat:** 12.6 g; **Trans Fat**: 0 g	
Protein: 5.6 g; **Total Carbs:** 68.7 g	
Dietary Fiber: 7.2 g; **Sugars:** 46.4 g	
Cholesterol: 0 mg; **Sodium:** 1035 mg; **Potassium**: 746 mg	
Vitamin A: 2%; **Vitamin C**: 45%; **Calcium**: 6%; **Iron**: 17%	
Good points: No cholesterol, high in manganese, very high in vitamin B6, and high in vitamin C.	

Ingredients:

- 8 ounces honey or smoked ham, diced (leftover ham will do)
- 4 parsnips, tops cut off, sliced
- 4 cloves garlic OR 1-1 1/2 teaspoon cloves garlic, minced
- 4 basil leaves, stems removed
- 2 tablespoons tapioca starch OR potato starch, for thickening
- 2 tablespoons sauce, gluten free soy OR tamari (if paleo or whole 30, coconut amino OR wine vinegar, dry white)
- 10 ounces coconut milk OR almond milk
- 1/2 teaspoon black pepper
- 1 teaspoon sea salt
- 1 tablespoon olive oil
- 1 sweet potato, large-sized, peeled, and sliced
- 1 cup onion, chopped
- 1 1/2-2 cups chicken broth- the less you use, the thicker the soup will be
- Extra olive, oil, herbs, coconut cream, and optional parmesan, for garnish/topping

- Extra salt and pepper, to taste

Directions:
1. Peel and then chop or slice the vegetables – onion, potato, and parsnips – and then put into the slow cooker. Pour the broth in the cooker. Add the 1/2 teaspoon of pepper, 1 teaspoon of salt, olive oil, garlic, and basil.
2. Close the lid of the cooker and cook for 2 hours on LOW or until the vegetables are tender.
3. Add the coconut/almond milk into the cooker. Using a hand blender, blend the mixture into the cooker until pureed and creamy.
4. Add the remaining ingredients – diced leftover ham, soy sauce/tamari, potato starch, extra pepper and salt to taste, and your choice of other seasoning. Mix to combine.
5. Close the lid of the cooker and cook for 1 hour on LOW.
6. Divide between bowls and serve drizzled with a small amount of milk/cream, olive oil, herbs, pepper, and optional parmesan.

Paleo Beef, Sweet Potato, and Carrot Stew

Prep Time: 10 minutes; **Cook Time:** 5 hours on HIGH

Serving Size: 329 g; **Serves:** 4; **Calories:** 391

Total Fat: 9 g **Saturated Fat**: 2.4 g; **Trans Fat**: 0 g

Protein: 47.9 g; **Total Carbs:** 23.3 g

Dietary Fiber: 4.8 g; **Sugars:** 9 g

Cholesterol: 113 mg; **Sodium**: 132 mg; **Potassium**: 1024 mg

Vitamin A: 259%; **Vitamin C**: 42%; **Calcium**: 5%; **Iron**: 37%

Good points: Low in sodium, high in selenium, very high in vitamin A, very high in vitamin B6, high in vitamin B12, high in vitamin C, high in zinc.

Ingredients:

- 500 grams steak, for braising
- 50 ml water
- 5 carrots, large-sized
- 2 tablespoons almond flour
- 2 sweet potatoes
- 100 ml red wine
- 1 teaspoon tomato puree
- 1 teaspoon olive oil
- 1 onion

Directions:

1. Preheat the slow cooker on HIGH setting for 20 minutes.
2. Trim any fat off from the meat and put in the cooker along with the olive and tomato puree.
3. Roughly chop the sweet potatoes, carrots, and onion, and add them into the cooker. Mix well.
4. Close the lid of the cooker and cook for 1 hour on HIGH. After 1 hour, add the red wine, then the water. Mix until well combined.

5. Close the lid of the cooker and cook for 4 hours on HIGH – stir every hour to prevent the stew from sticking to the cooker.
6. After 4 hours, the stew will be quite runny. Check the beef – if it is tender, then it is ready to serve.
7. Add 1 tablespoon of flour with just enough water to create a thick paste. Add the flour paste into the cooker very slowly – the stew will thicken quickly. Season with salt and pepper to taste, and serve.

Paleo Chicken Soup

Prep Time: 15 minutes; **Cook Time:** 6-8 hours on LOW

Serving Size: 348 g; **Serves:** 4-6; **Calories:** 198

Total Fat: 7.3 g **Saturated Fat**: 1.8 g; **Trans Fat**: 0 g

Protein: 24.4 g; **Total Carbs:** 7.8 g

Dietary Fiber: 2.7 g; **Sugars:** 3.7 g

Cholesterol: 69 mg; **Sodium**: 598 mg; **Potassium**: 415 mg

Vitamin A: 155%; **Vitamin C**: 8%; **Calcium**: 4%; **Iron**: 7%

Good points: High in niacin, high in selenium, very high in vitamin A, and high in vitamin B6.

Ingredients:
- 2 chicken thighs, organic, skin-on, bone-in
- 2 chicken breasts, organic, skin-on, bone-in
- 3 carrots, diced
- 1/2 teaspoon fresh ground pepper
- 1 teaspoon sea salt
- 1 teaspoon apple cider vinegar
- 1 tablespoon herbes de Provence OR several sprigs fresh herbs
- 1 onion, medium-sized, chopped
- 3 stalks celery, diced
- 3-4 cups filtered water

Directions:
1. Layer the ingredients in the slow cooker in the following order: onion, celery, carrots, apple cider vinegar, herbes de Provence, chicken breasts, chicken thighs, sea salt, and ground pepper. Pour in just enough water to cover the vegetables and come halfway up the chicken.
2. Close the lid of cooker and cook 6-8 hours on LOW.

3. When the cooking time is up, transfer the chicken into a clean cutting board. Remove the chicken and bones. Using 2 forks, shred the chicken meat and return into the cooker. Stir and adjust the seasonings. Reheat the soup and serve.

Paleo Chicken Fajita Soup

Prep Time: 15 minutes; **Cook Time:** 5-6 hours on LOW

Serving Size: 530 g; **Serves:** 6-8; **Calories:** 521

Total Fat: 18.7 g **Saturated Fat**: 4.5 g; **Trans Fat**: 0 g

Protein: 43.1 g; **Total Carbs:** 58.1 g

Dietary Fiber: 23.2 g; **Sugars:** 13.9 g

Cholesterol: 101 mg; **Sodium**: 861 mg; **Potassium**: 1792 mg

Vitamin A: 152%; **Vitamin C**: 160%; **Calcium**: 28%; **Iron**: 98%

Good points: High in dietary fiber, high in iron, high in manganese, high in niacin, very high in vitamin A, high in vitamin B6, and very high in vitamin C.

Ingredients:
- 1 1/2 pounds chicken breasts
- 1 1/2 teaspoon paprika
- 1 bay leaf
- 1 can (10 ounces) enchilada sauce, red
- 1 can (20 ounces) diced tomatoes, with juice
- 1 can (4 ounces) green chilies, chopped
- 1 jalapeno pepper, diced small
- 1 poblano pepper, diced, more to taste, optional
- 1 tablespoon chili powder
- 1 teaspoon cumin
- 1 teaspoon dried oregano
- 1 teaspoon onion powder
- 1 yellow onion, large-sized, chopped small
- 1/2 green AND 1/2 red bell peppers, diced
- 1/2 teaspoon cayenne
- 1/2 teaspoon ground black pepper
- 1/2 teaspoon salt
- 1/4 cup cilantro leaves, chopped small
- 1-2 avocados, cubed, for topping
- 2 limes, juice only

- 3 cloves garlic, minced
- 4 cups chicken stock

Directions:
1. Except for the avocado, cilantro, and lime juice, put the rest of the ingredients into the slow cooker and mix to combine.
2. Close the lid of the cooker and cook for 5-6 hours on LOW.
3. After cooking time taste the seasoning and adjust as needed. When the chicken is cooked – the internal temperature should be 160F – remove from the cooker, shred using 2 forks, and then return the shredded chicken meat into the cooker.
4. Just before serving remove the bay leaf and discard. Add the cilantro and lime juice.
5. Divide the soup between bowls and top each serving with avocado slices.

Paleo Nourishing Chicken Soup

Prep Time: 45 minutes; **Cook Time:** 6 hours on HIGH, plus 10 minutes reheating

Serving Size: 314 g; **Serves**: 8; **Calories:** 397

Total Fat: 11.1 g **Saturated Fat:** 3.1 g; **Trans Fat**: 0 g

Protein: 59.9 g; **Total Carbs:** 11.2 g

Dietary Fiber: 2.5 g; **Sugars:** 3.4 g

Cholesterol: 168 mg; **Sodium:** 1725 mg; **Potassium:** 816 mg

Vitamin A: 295%; **Vitamin C**: 75%; **Calcium**: 11%; **Iron**: 22%

Good points: Low in sugar, very high in niacin, high in phosphorus, high in selenium, very high in vitamin A, high in vitamin B6, and high in vitamin C.

Ingredients:

- 1 pound carrots, peeled, sliced lengthwise into halves and cut into 1/4-inch slices
- 2 pounds chicken thighs, skin removed, bone-in (about 5 thighs)
- 2 cloves garlic, minced
- 1/4 teaspoon pepper
- 1/2 tablespoon real salt
- 1/2 tablespoon fresh thyme, chopped
- 1/2 bunch kale, stems removed and chopped into bite-sized pieces (about 4 cups packed)
- 1 yellow onion, diced
- 2 sprigs fresh thyme
- 2 tablespoons chicken base (if using water instead of chicken broth)
- 5 cups chicken OR stock water
- Real salt and pepper, to taste

Directions:

1. Put the chicken thighs on the bottom of the slow cooker. Sprinkle both sides of the meat with pepper and salt.
2. Put the garlic and thyme sprigs on top of the chicken thighs. Pour the chicken broth/water into the cooker. If using, add the chicken base.
3. Close the lid of the cooker and cook for 4 hours on HIGH.
4. After cooking time is complete, the chicken should be fall-off-the-bone tender. Carefully remove the chicken and transfer into a bowl.
5. Remove the thyme sprig from the cooker and discard.
6. At this point, if desired, strain the broth through a fine mesh strainer to remove any chicken debris. If straining, return the broth into the cooker. Set the slow cooker to HIGH setting.
7. Separate the chicken meat from the bones and lightly shred the meat using 2 forks. Discard any cartilage.
8. Add the chicken bones into the cooker. Cover the bowl with the chicken meat and refrigerate.
9. Add the thyme, onions, and carrots into the cooker. Close the lid and cook for 2 hours on HIGH. In the last 30 minutes of cooking, add the kale. After 2 hours, the carrots and kale should be tender and soft.
10. Remove the chicken bones from the soup and discard.
11. Taste the soup and adjust the seasoning as needed.
12. Add the shredded chicken meat and reheat for about 10 minutes – do not stir too much or the chicken will be over-shredded. Serve.

Paleo Slow Cooked Meatball Soup

Prep Time: 10 minutes; **Cook Time:** 2 hours on HIGH

Serving Size: 589 g; **Serves**: 2; **Calories:** 542

Total Fat: 16.3 g **Saturated Fat**: 6 g; **Trans Fat**: 0 g

Protein: 79.3 g; **Total Carbs:** 17.2 g

Dietary Fiber: 5 g; **Sugars:** 9.6 g

Cholesterol: 223 mg; **Sodium**: 184 mg; **Potassium**: 1779 mg

Vitamin A: 40%; **Vitamin C**: 73%; **Calcium**: 6%; **Iron**: 269%

Good points: Low in sodium, very high in iron, high in niacin, high in phosphorus, very high in selenium, very high in vitamin B6, very high in vitamin B12, high in vitamin C, and very high in zinc.

Ingredients:
- 250 ml tomato, preferably homemade
- 2 tomatoes, large-sized, diced
- 100 grams courgette/zucchini
- 1 onion, large-sized, diced

For the Meatballs:
- 500 grams beef, minced
- 25 grams onion, diced
- 1 teaspoon tomato puree
- 1 teaspoon oregano
- 1 teaspoon basil
- Salt and pepper

Directions:
1. Put all of the meatball ingredients into a bowl and mix until combined. Form the meat mixture into 12 medium-sized balls and set aside.

2. Fill the slow cooker with whatever vegetable you decided to use. Pour the tomato sauce into the cooker and mix well.
3. Lay the meatballs on top of the vegetable mixture.
4. Close the lid of the cooker and for 2 hours on HIGH.
5. Divide between bowls and top each serving with a bit of coconut milk and fresh chives.

Apple Butternut Soup with Crispy Leeks

Prep Time: 25 minutes; **Cook Time:** 8 hours on LOW; 5 hours on HIGH		

Prep Time: 25 minutes; **Cook Time:** 8 hours on LOW; 5 hours on HIGH

Serving Size: 497 g; **Serves:** 4; **Calories:** 270

Total Fat: 11.8 g **Saturated Fat**: 9.6 g; **Trans Fat**: 0 g

Protein: 6.80 g; **Total Carbs:** 39.8 g

Dietary Fiber: 6.7 g; **Sugars:** 11.9 g

Cholesterol: 0 mg; **Sodium**: 567 mg; **Potassium**: 1154 mg

Vitamin A: 546%; **Vitamin C**: 92%; **Calcium**: 15%; **Iron**: 18%

Good points: No cholesterol, high in manganese, high in potassium, very high in vitamin A, and very high in vitamin C.

Ingredients:

For the soup:

- 2 pounds butternut squash, peeled, seeded and cubed (about 1/2 medium-sized butternut squash)
- 2 1/2 cups vegetable broth
- 1/2 cup coconut milk, canned
- 1 leek, white parts only, rinsed well and then roughly chopped
- 1 Granny Smith apple, medium-sized, unpeeled or peeled, roughly chopped
- 1 carrot, medium-sized, roughly chopped

For garnish:

- 3/4 cup leeks, white parts only, thinly sliced, rinsed well
- 1/8 teaspoon sea salt
- 1 tablespoon coconut oil OR other high heat oil
- Coconut milk, for drizzling, optional

Directions:

For the soup:

1. Put the carrot, squash, apple, leek, and pour the broth in the slow cooker.
2. Close the lid of the cooker and cook for 8 hours on LOW or for 5 hours on HIGH.
3. After cooking time, stir the coconut milk in the soup mix. With an immersion or a stand blender, puree the soup.

For the garnish:
1. Put a medium-sized, nonstick skillet on the stovetop and heat to medium-low heat. Add the oil in the skillet and then the leeks. Cook for about 10 minutes, occasionally stirring, until crisp and golden. Season with salt.

To assemble:
1. Divide the soup between 6 bowls. Garnish each serving with crispy leeks. Drizzle with extra coconut milk, if desired.

Paleo Tortilla Chicken Soup

Prep Time: 30 minutes; **Cook Time:** 2 hours on LOW

Serving Size: 485 g; **Serves**: 6; **Calories:** 196

Total Fat: 5.7 g **Saturated Fat**: 1.5 g; **Trans Fat**: 0 g

Protein: 21.9 g; **Total Carbs:** 14.5 g

Dietary Fiber: 4.1 g; **Sugars:** 7.8 g

Cholesterol: 50 mg; **Sodium**: 724 mg; **Potassium**: 911 mg

Vitamin A: 157%; **Vitamin C**: 43%; **Calcium**: 7%; **Iron**: 12%

Good points: very high in niacin, high in phosphorus, high in potassium, high in selenium, very high in vitamin A, high in vitamin B6, and very high in vitamin C.

Ingredients:

- 2 cups celery, chopped
- 2 cups carrots, shredded
- 2 chicken breasts, large-sized, skin removed and then cut into 1/2-inch strips
- 1 can (28 ounces) diced tomatoes
- 1 sweet onion, diced
- 1 teaspoon chili powder
- 1 teaspoon cumin
- 1-2 cups water
- 1 bunch cilantro, finely chopped
- 2 jalapeno peppers, seeded and diced
- 2 tablespoons tomato paste
- 32 ounces chicken broth, organic
- 4 cloves garlic, minced
- Olive oil
- Sea salt and fresh ground pepper, to taste

Directions:

1. Put a dash of oil in a skillet over medium-high heat. Add about 1/4 cup of chicken broth. Add

the jalapeno, garlic, onion, pepper, and sea salt and cook until the vegetables are soft – add more broth into the skillet as needed.

2. Transfer the jalapeno mixture into the slow cooker. Add the rest of the ingredients in the cooker and pour in just enough water to fill the cooker.

3. Close the lid of the cooker and cook for 2 hours on LOW. After cooking time, taste and adjust seasoning as needed. Using 2 forks or tongs, shred the chicken. Divide the soup between bowls and to each serving with slices of avocado and fresh cilantro.

Fish and Seafood

Paleo Moqueca Brazilian White Fish Stew

Prep Time: 15 minutes; **Cook Time:** 4 hours on LOW

Serving Size: 1512 g; **Serves**: 2; **Calories**: 1062

Total Fat: 36.5 g **Saturated Fat**: 28 g; **Trans Fat**: 0 g

Protein: 127.8 g; **Total Carbs:** 62.4 g

Dietary Fiber: 18.4 g; **Sugars:** 38.2 g

Cholesterol: 275 mg; **Sodium**: 2573 mg; **Potassium**: 4255 mg

Vitamin A: 655%; **Vitamin C**: 345%; **Calcium**: 26%; **Iron**: 66%

Good points: High in potassium, very high in selenium, very high in vitamin A, high in vitamin B6, and very high in vitamin C.

Ingredients:
- 1 kilogram white fish
- 1 red pepper, small-sized, diced
- 1 tablespoon garlic puree
- 1 tablespoon paprika
- 1 teaspoon rosemary
- 250 ml coconut milk
- 3 tablespoons coriander

For the sauce:
- 1 courgette/zucchini, medium-sized
- 1 teaspoon coriander
- 1 teaspoon garlic puree
- 1 teaspoon thyme
- 3 tomatoes, large-sized
- 5 carrots, large-sized, peeled
- 750 ml tomato sauce, preferably homemade
- Salt and pepper

Directions:

1. Put the carrot, courgette, and tomatoes into the slow cooker, chopping them as you go. Add the tomato sauce, and 1 teaspoon each of salt, pepper, thyme, coriander, and garlic puree. Stir until well mixed.
2. Close the lid of the cooker and cook for 2 hours on LOW.
3. Add the white fish into the cooker and as you add the fish, season with pepper, salt, and garlic puree, seasoning the fish as it goes in.
4. Close the lid of the cooker and cook for 1 hour on LOW or until the fish is 75% cooked.
5. After cooking time, drain excess tomato sauce - the stew will be very runny, depending on how watery the white fish is.
6. Add the coconut milk into the cooker and stir well to mix.
7. Add the remaining seasoning, a bit more black pepper, salt, and red pepper. Close the lid of the cooker and cook for 1 hour on LOW.

Lemon and Dill Salmon

Prep Time: 5 minutes; **Cook Time:** 1-2 hours on HIGH

Serving Size: 272 g; **Serves**: 2; **Calories:** 353

Total Fat: 15.7 g **Saturated Fat**: 27 g; **Trans Fat**: 0 g

Protein: 46.9 g; **Total Carbs:** 10.4 g

Dietary Fiber: 2.5 g; **Sugars:** 0.8 g

Cholesterol: 103 mg; **Sodium**: 126 mg; **Potassium**: 1321 mg

Vitamin A: 19%; **Vitamin C**: 37%; **Calcium**: 31%; **Iron**: 42%

Good points: Low in sodium, very low in sugar, high in iron, very high in magnesium, very high in phosphorus, high in potassium, very high in selenium, and high in vitamin C.

Ingredients:
- 1-2 pounds salmon
- 1/2 teaspoon ghee, optional
- 1 lemon, sliced
- 2 garlic cloves, minced
- Handful fresh dill
- Salt and pepper, to taste

Directions:
1. Line the slow cooker with parchment paper.
2. Season the salmon with pepper, salt, fresh dill, and garlic.
3. Put the lemon on top of the parchment paper. Top the salmon with the ghee and lemon slices.
4. Close the lid of the cooker and cook for 1-2 hours on HIGH.
5. After the cooking time, lift out the parchment paper to serve the salmon.

Notes: You do not need to add water to cook this dish. If cooking it without water is uncomfortable for you, then add 2-4 tablespoons of water on the parchment paper before putting the fish on.

Paleo Parsley Lemon-Orange Fish

Prep Time: 10 minutes; **Cook Time:** 1 1/2 hours on LOW	

Serving Size: 410 g; **Serves**: 2; **Calories:** 900	
Total Fat: 51.3 g **Saturated Fat**: 10.9 g; **Trans Fat**: 0 g	
Protein: 50.7 g; **Total Carbs:** 65.4 g	
Dietary Fiber: 4.3 g; **Sugars:** 1.5 g	
Cholesterol: 116 mg; **Sodium**: 1814 mg; **Potassium**: 1200 mg	
Vitamin A: 10%; **Vitamin C**: 56%; **Calcium**: 10%; **Iron**: 43%	
Good points: Very low in sugar.	

Ingredients:
- 1 1/2 pounds fish fillet (I used cod)
- 1/2 onion, chopped
- 2 tablespoons parsley
- 4 teaspoons olive oil
- 1 lemon, grated rind
- 1 orange, grated rind
- Dash of salt and pepper

Directions:
1. Butter the slow cooker.
2. Put the fish in the cooker and put the rest of the ingredients on top of the fish.
3. Close the lid of the cooker and cook for 1 1/2 hours on LOW. Enjoy!

Fish Fillets Poached in Coconut Milk

Prep Time: 10 minutes; **Cook Time:** 1 hour on HIGH

Serving Size: 773 g; **Serves**: 4; **Calories:** 1665

Total Fat: 154.7 g **Saturated Fat**: 127.8 g; **Trans Fat**: 0 g

Protein: 55.4 g; **Total Carbs:** 33.7 g

Dietary Fiber: 13.2 g; **Sugars:** 19.9 g

Cholesterol: 131mg; **Sodium**: 1966 mg; **Potassium**: 2269 mg

Vitamin A: 5%; **Vitamin C**: 30%; **Calcium**: 16%; **Iron**: 59%

Good points: High in manganese.

Ingredients:
- 4 pieces (about 6 ounces each) white fish fillets,
- 1/2 teaspoon salt for every coconut milk can
- Several cans of coconut milk (regular and not light), to cover the fish fillets while poaching
- Your choice of aromatics - garlic, parsley, shallots, ginger, capers, lemon, etc.

Directions:
1. With the skin side faced down, put the fish fillets in the slow cooker.
2. Add all of the aromatics in the cooker – evenly distribute them on top and around the fish.
3. Heat the coconut milk on a stovetop or in a microwave. Pour into the cooker.
4. Close the lid of the cooker and cook for 1 hour on HIGH or until the fish is opaque.
5. Serve garnished with aromatics, if desired. You can also add extra lemon for serving. Serve immediately.

Slow Cooked Mediterranean Salmon

Prep Time: 20 minutes; **Cook Time:** 6 hours on LOW

Serving Size: 229 g; **Serves:** 4; **Calories:** 225

Total Fat: 11.8 g **Saturated Fat**: 1.7 g; **Trans Fat**: 0 g

Protein: 23.5 g; **Total Carbs:** 8 g

Dietary Fiber: 1.6 g; **Sugars:** 4 g

Cholesterol: 52 mg; **Sodium**: 350 mg; **Potassium**: 704 mg

Vitamin A: 26%; **Vitamin C**: 117%; **Calcium**: 6%; **Iron**: 7%

Good points: Very high in magnesium; very high in phosphorus, very high in selenium, high in vitamin A, and very high in vitamin C.

Ingredients:
- 1 pound salmon fillets
- 1 zucchini, quartered and then sliced
- 1 tomato, chopped
- 1 teaspoon onion powder, divided
- 1 teaspoon garlic powder, divided
- 1 tablespoon olive oil, divided
- 1 tablespoon Italian seasoning, divided
- 1 red bell pepper, julienned
- 1/2 teaspoon kosher salt, divided
- 1/2 onion, sliced
- 1/2 teaspoon black pepper, divided
- 3 cloves garlic, sliced

Directions:
1. Get an on oval-shaped, oven-proof dish, such as Pyrex, that will fit inside a 6-quart slow cooker. Grease the dish well with nonstick cooking spray. Put the salmon in the dish and season the fish with half of the olive oil, black pepper, Italian seasoning, onion powder, garlic powder, and salt.

81

2. Add the tomato, bell pepper, zucchini, onion, and garlic, and season with the remaining olive oil, herbs, and spices. Gently toss the veggies to coat.
3. Cover the dish with the glass lid, if it has one. If not, cover with aluminum foil. Put the dish in the cooker and close the lid of the cooker. Cook for 6 hours on LOW or until the salmon is cooked through and easily flakes. Serve with couscous or whole-grain pasta.

Notes: If you do not have a dish, then just wrap everything with foil and put in the slow cooker.

Salmon Poached in Pomegranate

Prep Time: 20 minutes; **Cook Time:** 1 hour on HIGH	

Prep Time: 20 minutes; **Cook Time:** 1 hour on HIGH

Serving Size: 486 g; **Serves:** 4; **Calories:** 429

Total Fat: 14.4 g **Saturated Fat**: 2 g; **Trans Fat**: 0 g

Protein: 35.1 g; **Total Carbs:** 43.3 g

Dietary Fiber: 5 g; **Sugars:** 31.6 g

Cholesterol: 75 mg; **Sodium**: 113 mg; **Potassium**: 1458 mg

Vitamin A: 11%; **Vitamin C**: 104%; **Calcium**: 15%; **Iron**: 12%

Good points: Low in sodium, high in magnesium, very high in phosphorus, very high in selenium, and very high in vitamin C.

Ingredients:
- 4 pieces (6-oz each) wild salmon fillets, skinless or skin-on
- 4 lemon slices, thin pieces
- 2 teaspoons allspice, whole berries
- 2 tablespoons fresh mint, chopped
- 2 oranges
- 2 cups pomegranate juice, 100%
- 1/8 teaspoon black pepper, fresh ground
- 1/4 cup pomegranate arils
- 1/2 cup red onion, thinly sliced
- 1 tablespoon white wine vinegar
- 1 tablespoon raw honey
- 1 tablespoon extra-virgin olive oil
- 1 fennel bulb, large-sized, fronds trimmed and thinly sliced

Directions:
1. Put the pomegranate juice, honey, and 1 cup of water into a 5-6 quart slow cooker and stir to combine. Add the allspice.

2. Close the lid of the cooker cook for 30 minutes on HIGH.
3. After 30 minutes, add the salmon to the cooker and put the lemon slices on top of the fish. Close the lid of the cooker and cook for 20-30 minutes on HIGH or until the center of the salmon is opaque.
4. Meanwhile, prepare the salad. In a large-sized bowl, combine the onion and the fennel. Slice a thin layer off the bottom and the top of 1 orange. With a cut side faced down, place the orange on a cutting board. Using a paring knife, remove the peel, following the curve of the orange. Transfer the orange into a wide, shallow bowl and discard the peel.
5. Carefully cut along the membranes toward the center of the orange to separate the segments. Repeat the process with the remaining orange.
6. Add the juices and the orange segments into the onion mixture. Add the pomegranate arils, oil, and vinegar. Toss to combine and season with pepper.
7. Divide the salmon and the salad between serving plates.

Garlicky Shrimp

Prep Time: 30 minutes; **Cook Time:** 40 minutes on HIGH	
Serving Size: 183 g; **Serves:** 6-8; **Calories:** 402	
Total Fat: 27.8 g **Saturated Fat:** 4.4 g; **Trans Fat:** 0 g	
Protein: 34.7 g; **Total Carbs:** 3.6 g	
Dietary Fiber: 0 g; **Sugars:** 0 g	
Cholesterol: 318 mg; **Sodium:** 758 mg; **Potassium:** 283 mg	
Vitamin A: 15%; **Vitamin C:** 4%; **Calcium:** 14%; **Iron:** 4%	
Good points: Very low in sugar, high in phosphorus, and high in vitamin B12.	

Ingredients:
- 2 pounds raw shrimp, extra-large-sized (26-30 count), peeled and then deveined
- 1/4 teaspoon crushed red pepper flakes
- 1/4 teaspoon black pepper, freshly ground
- 1 teaspoon smoked Spanish paprika (pimenton OR sweet paprika)
- 1 teaspoon kosher salt
- 1 tablespoon flat-leaf parsley, minced, for garnish
- 3/4 cup extra-virgin olive oil
- 6 cloves garlic, thinly sliced

Directions:
1. Put the red pepper flakes, black pepper, salt, paprika, garlic, and oil into a 5-6 quart slow cooker and stir until well blended. Close the lid of cooker and cook for 30 minutes on HIGH.
2. Stir in the shrimp and stir to coat evenly. Close the lid of the cooker and cook for 10 minutes on HIGH. Stir to make sure the shrimps are cooking evenly. Close the lid of the cooker and

cook for 10 minutes on HIGH or until all the shrimps are just opaque.

3. Transfer the shrimp and some of the sauce into a wide, shallow serving dish. Sprinkle with parsley and serve while still warm.

Sausage, Shrimp, Kale, and Black-Eyed Peas

Prep Time: 30 minutes; **Cook Time:** 6-8 hours on LOW; 3-4 hours on HIGH, plus 30 minutes on HIGH	

Serving Size: 656 g; **Serves**: 4-6; **Calories:** 621
Total Fat: 21.3 g **Saturated Fat**: 6 g; **Trans Fat**: 0 g
Protein: 54.2 g; **Total Carbs:** 56.3 g
Dietary Fiber: 14.1 g; **Sugars:** 8.2 g
Cholesterol: 286 mg; **Sodium:** 1049 mg; **Potassium**: 1432 mg
Vitamin A: 411%; **Vitamin C**: 313%; **Calcium**: 38%; **Iron**: 49%
Good points: High in thiamin, very high in vitamin A, and very high in vitamin C.

Ingredients:
- 1/2 pound Italian turkey sausage, casings removed
- 2 cans (15-ounce) black-eyed peas, rinsed and then drained
- 1 can (14 1/2-ounce) crushed tomatoes
- 1 pound kale, trimmed and then coarsely chopped
- 1 pound shrimp, large-sized, peeled and then deveined
- 1/2 cup sliced roasted red peppers, drained
- 1 tablespoon fresh oregano, chopped OR 1 teaspoon dried
- 1 tablespoon paprika
- 1 teaspoon extra-virgin olive oil
- 1 Vidalia onion, chopped
- 1/4 teaspoon red pepper flakes
- 3 garlic cloves, minced

Directions:

1. Put the oil in a large-sized skillet and heat on medium-high heat. Add the sausage, garlic, and onion. Cook for about 10 minutes, breaking up the sausage in the process using a wooden spoon, until the sausage is browned.
2. Add the tomatoes, red pepper flakes, and paprika. Bring the mixture to a boil, stirring and scraping the browned bits off from the bottom of the skillet.
3. Transfer the sausage mix into a 5-6 quart slow cooker. Add the black-eyed peas and kale. Stir until well mixed.
4. Close the lid of the cooker and cook for about 6-8 hours on LOW or for 3-4 hours on HIGH.
5. Add the roasted red peppers, shrimp, and oregano. Mix until well combined.
6. Close the lid of the cooker and cook for 30 minutes on HIGH or until the center of the shrimps are just opaque.

Braised Sea Bass and Vegetables

Prep Time: 30 minutes; **Cook Time:** 2 1/2 hours on LOW; 1 1/2 hours on HIGH

Serving Size: 385 g; **Serves:** 6; **Calories:** 630

Total Fat: 32.8 g **Saturated Fat:** 7.1 g; **Trans Fat:** 0 g

Protein: 35.1 g; **Total Carbs:** 53.5 g

Dietary Fiber: 5.1 g; **Sugars:** 3.2 g

Cholesterol: 77 mg; **Sodium:** 1277 mg; **Potassium:** 1227 mg

Vitamin A: 121%; **Vitamin C:** 28%; **Calcium:** 12%; **Iron:** 36%

Good points: Low in sugar and high in vitamin A.

Ingredients:
- 6 fillets (about 2-3 pounds) sea bass OR other firm-fleshed white fish
- 3 leeks, large-sized, cleaned and then thinly sliced
- 3 carrots, large-sized, julienned
- 2 tablespoons of butter or olive oil
- 2 bulbs fennel, thinly sliced
- Salt and black pepper

Directions:
1. Put the butter in a large-sized skillet and melt over medium heat. Add the carrots, leeks, and fennel. Cook, frequently stirring until starting to become soft and slightly browned. Season with salt and pepper. Transfer 1/2 of the carrot mix into the bottom of the slow cooker.
2. Season the sea bass with pepper and salt and put on top of the veggie mix in the cooker. Top the sea bass with the remaining 1/2 of the carrot mix.

3. Close the lid of the cooker and cook for 2 1/2 hours on LOW or for 1 1/2 hours on HIGH or until the fish is cooked through.

Slow Cooker Crock Pot Greek Fish Stew

Prep Time: 15 minutes; **Cook Time:** 4-6 hours on HIGH

Serving Size: 777 g; **Serves**: 5; **Calories**: 396

Total Fat: 15.2 g **Saturated Fat**: 2.6 g; **Trans Fat**: 0 g

Protein: 49 g; **Total Carbs:** 15.3 g

Dietary Fiber: 4.4 g; **Sugars:** 6.9 g

Cholesterol: 122 mg; **Sodium**: 717 mg; **Potassium**: 1770 mg

Vitamin A: 96%; **Vitamin C**: 72%; **Calcium**: 14%; **Iron**: 18%

Good points: High in niacin, very high in phosphorus, high in potassium, high in selenium, very high in vitamin A, high in vitamin B6, high in vitamin B12, and high in vitamin C.

Ingredients:
- 5 white fish fillets, large-sized
- 4 cloves garlic
- 3 stalks celery, chopped
- 1/2 teaspoon saffron threads
- 1 onion, large-sized
- 1 lemon, zested and juiced
- 1 leek, sliced
- 1 carrot, chopped
- 1 can tomatoes
- 8 cups vegetable or fish stock
- Handful mint leaves, chopped
- Handful parsley leaves, chopped

Directions:
1. Put all of the ingredients into the slow cooker.
2. Close the lid of the cooker and cook for 4-6 hours on HIGH.
3. Serve with Paleo bread.

Meat

Pineapple Pork Ribs

Prep Time: 15 minutes; **Cook Time:** 7-8 hours on LOW	

Prep Time: 15 minutes; **Cook Time:** 7-8 hours on LOW

Serving Size: 727 g; **Serves**: 4-6; **Calories:** 1081

Total Fat: 63.2 g **Saturated Fat**: 22 g; **Trans Fat**: 0 g

Protein: 93.3 g; **Total Carbs:** 33 g

Dietary Fiber: 5.9 g; **Sugars:** 22.3 g

Cholesterol: 355 mg; **Sodium**: 216 mg; **Potassium**: 1695 mg

Vitamin A: 41%; **Vitamin C**: 184%; **Calcium**: 20%; **Iron**: 36%

Good points: Low in sodium, high in manganese, very high in selenium, high in thiamin, and high in vitamin C.

Ingredients:
- 3 pounds baby back pork ribs
- 2 tablespoons Italian seasoning
- 2 tablespoons dried rosemary
- 2 tablespoons dried basil
- 2 cloves garlic, minced, optional, (omit for low FODMAPs)
- 1 teaspoon sea salt
- 1 cup green onion, chopped OR 1 white onion, chopped (use green onion for low FODMAP)
- 4 heaping cups fresh pineapple, chopped
- 6 tomatoes, medium-sized, chopped

Directions:
1. Set the slow cooker to LOW setting.
2. Put all of the ingredients into the slow cooker.
3. Close the lid of the cooker and cook for 7-8 hours - you can stir every couple of hours to distribute the sauce evenly. Enjoy!

Kalua Pig

Prep Time: 10 minutes; **Cook Time:** 16 hours on LOW	
Serving Size: 295 g; **Serves:** 8; **Calories:** 869	
Total Fat: 63.6 g **Saturated Fat:** 23.3 g; **Trans Fat:** 0 g	
Protein: 68.8 g; **Total Carbs:** 0.7 g	
Dietary Fiber: 0 g; **Sugars:** 0 g	
Cholesterol: 263 mg; **Sodium:** 1411 mg; **Potassium:** 981 mg	
Vitamin A: 1%; **Vitamin C:** 3%; **Calcium:** 7%; **Iron:** 22%	
Good points: Very low in sugar, high in selenium, and high in thiamin.	

Ingredients:
- 1 piece (5-pound) pork shoulder roast, bone-in or out
- 3 slices bacon
- 5 cloves garlic, optional
- 1 1/2 tablespoons coarse sea salt (I used Alaea Hawaiian)

Directions:
1. Line the bottom of the slow cooker with the slices of bacon. If you don't have bacon, just rub the surface of the pork with 2 teaspoons of smoked paprika to replicate the smoky flavor – bacon does make it better, though.
2. If desired, cut 5 small-sized incisions in the pork and tuck cloves of garlic inside. Season the pork with salt – make sure to season all the nooks and crannies.
3. With the skin side faced up, put the pork in the slow cooker.
4. Close the lid of the cooker and cook for 16 hours on LOW or until the meat is fork tender.
5. When the pork is cooked, transfer into a platter and shred – do not shred in the cooker; the

cooking liquid will make your meat too salty. Season the shredded meat with some of the cooking liquid to taste. Serve as is. Fill a crisp lettuce for lettuce tacos and top with guacamole and tomatoes. Toss with a summer salad or wrap in toasted sheets of nori.

Paleo Meatloaf

Prep Time: 30 minutes; **Cook Time:** 4-6 hours on LOW

Serving Size: 230 g; **Serves**: 6; **Calories:** 409

Total Fat: 19.3 g **Saturated Fat**: 7.6 g; **Trans Fat**: 0 g

Protein: 49.9 g; **Total Carbs:** 5.8 g

Dietary Fiber: 1.9 g; **Sugars:** 1.9 g

Cholesterol: 190 mg; **Sodium**: 676 mg; **Potassium**: 817 mg

Vitamin A: 20%; **Vitamin C**: 9%; **Calcium**: 5%; **Iron**: 34%

Good points: Low in sugar, high in niacin, high in phosphorus, very high in selenium, high in vitamin B6, high in vitamin B12, and high in zinc.

Ingredients:
- 4 ounces bacon, crisped and then chopped
- 2 pounds lean ground meat (ground chicken or turkey)
- 2 eggs, beaten
- 4 green onions, chopped
- 2 teaspoons smoked paprika
- 2 teaspoons garlic powder
- 2 teaspoons dried oregano
- 2 stalks celery, chopped or sliced thinly
- 1/2 white onion, small-sized, diced small
- 1 teaspoon thyme
- 1 teaspoon black pepper

For the tomato sauce:
- 1/4 cup tomato sauce
- 1 teaspoon apple cider vinegar
- 2 teaspoons garlic powder
- 2 teaspoons smoked paprika
- 2-3 tablespoons Dijon mustard

Directions:

1. In a skillet, cook the bacon until crispy and brown. When cooked, crumble the bacon.
2. In a large-sized bowl, combine the ground meat with the crumbled bacon, beaten eggs, vegetables, and seasoning. With clean hands, mix until combined and form into a loaf.
3. Put the loaf into the slow cooker. Press it down to flatten the top – there should be 1 inch of space between the sides of the cooker and the meatloaf.
4. Mix the tomato sauce ingredients until well combined and spoon over the meat loaf. With a knife or a spoon, frost the top of the loaf as evenly as you can.
5. Close the lid of the cooker and cook for 4-6 hours on LOW.

Paleo Meatballs In Marinara Sauce

Prep Time: 15 minutes; **Cook Time:** 4 hours on LOW

Serving Size: 332 g; **Serves**: 6-8; **Calories:** 286

Total Fat: 8.6 g **Saturated Fat**: 2.4 g; **Trans Fat**: 0 g

Protein: 30.3 g; **Total Carbs:** 23.5 g

Dietary Fiber: 7.7 g; **Sugars:** 13.9 g

Cholesterol: 96 mg; **Sodium**: 621 mg; **Potassium**: 854 mg

Vitamin A: 51%; **Vitamin C**: 47%; **Calcium**: 13%; **Iron**: 102%

Good points: High in dietary fiber, very high in iron, high in selenium, high in vitamin A, very high in vitamin B6, very high in vitamin B12, high in vitamin C, and high in zinc.

Ingredients:
For the meatballs:
- 1-3/4 pounds ground beef, 85% lean
- 1/4 cup almond flour, blanched
- 1/2 teaspoon garlic powder
- 1 tablespoon Italian seasoning blend
- 1 tablespoon fresh parsley, chopped, optional
- 1 egg
- 2 teaspoons onion powder
- 3/4 teaspoon sea salt, fine grain, divided
- Generous pinch crushed red pepper, less or more to taste

For the sauce:
- 1 can (14 ounces) diced tomatoes with garlic and basil
- 1 can (28 ounces) crushed tomatoes with basil
- 1 can (6 ounces) tomato paste
- 1/2 onion, medium-sized, chopped
- 2 bay leaves
- 2 tablespoons fresh garlic, chopped

- 2 tablespoons fresh oregano leaves, chopped
- Sea salt, to taste

Directions:
For the meatballs:

1. In a small-sized bowl, mix the almond flour with the crushed red pepper, Italian seasoning, garlic powder, onion, and 1/2 teaspoon of sea salt.
2. In a large-sized bowl, add the ground beef and evenly season with the remaining sea salt.
3. Add the almond flour, egg, and, if using, parsley. With clean hands, mix until the ingredients are evenly distributed and the mixture bind – do not overmix or the meatballs will become tough.
4. Line a large-sized baking sheet with parchment paper and then preheat the broiler. Form the meat mixture into 20 meatballs and arrange onto the baking sheet.
5. Broil for about 2-4 minutes or until slightly browned and a small amount of fat is released. Immediately remove from the broiler.
6. Put the slightly browned meatballs into the slow cooker – leave behind any fat rendered in the baking sheet. Pour the sauce ingredients over the meatballs and gently stir to coat with the sauce – be careful not to break the meatballs.
7. Close the lid of the cooker and cook for 4 hours on LOW or until the meatballs are cooked through.
8. Serve with desired accompaniments and garnish with your favorite fresh herbs.

Notes: You can serve this with zucchini or sweet potato noodles, or with your favorite roasted vegetables or eggs. Store leftovers for up to 4 days in the fridge or in the fridge for up to 1 month.

Slow cookers are different. You can check at 3 1/2 hours of cooking time. Do not cook the meatballs for more than 4 1/2-5 hours or the meatballs will become dry and overcooked.

Paleo Pot

Prep Time: 5 minutes; **Cook Time:** 2-3 hour on HIGH

Serving Size: 414 g; **Serves:** 4; **Calories:** 339

Total Fat: 7.5 g **Saturated Fat:** 2.7 g; **Trans Fat:** 0 g

Protein: 38.1 g; **Total Carbs:** 29.7 g

Dietary Fiber: 7 g; **Sugars:** 6.2 g

Cholesterol: 101 mg; **Sodium:** 116 mg; **Potassium:** 1471 mg

Vitamin A: 130%; **Vitamin C:** 74%; **Calcium:** 7%; **Iron:** 128%

Good points: Low in sodium, very high in iron, high in phosphorus, high in potassium, high in selenium, very high in vitamin A, very high in vitamin B6, very high in vitamin B12, very high in vitamin C, and high in zinc.

Ingredients:
- 1 pound meat, browned
- 1 onion, medium-sized, chopped
- 1 teaspoon Flavor God's garlic and herb salt
- 1 teaspoon Flavor God's no salt
- 1 zucchini, spiralized
- 1/2 pound green beans
- 1/2 pound sweet potatoes, peeled and then chopped
- 1/4 cup fresh parsley
- 1/4 cup water
- 2 carrots, medium-sized, hopped
- 2 Roma tomatoes, chopped

Directions:
1. Put all of the ingredients into the slow cooker. Stir until well mixed.
2. Close the lid of the cooker and cook for 2-3 hour on HIGH or until the veggies are soft.

Paleo Meatloaf with Potatoes

Prep Time: 10 minutes; **Cook Time:** 3 hours

Serving Size: 267 g; **Serves**: 6; **Calories:** 269

Total Fat: 9.4 g **Saturated Fat**: 2.5 g; **Trans Fat**: 0 g

Protein: 27.3 g; **Total Carbs:** 19.3 g

Dietary Fiber: 3.3 g; **Sugars:** 4.9 g

Cholesterol: 99 mg; **Sodium**: 657 mg; **Potassium**: 952 mg

Vitamin A: 14%; **Vitamin C**: 28%; **Calcium**: 4%; **Iron**: 88%

Good points: Very high in iron, high in phosphorus, high in selenium, very high in vitamin B6, very high in vitamin B12, high in vitamin C, and high in zinc.

Ingredients:
- 1 pound ground meat
- 1 pound fingerling potatoes
- 1 onion, small-sized, diced
- 1 egg, small-sized
- 1 teaspoon Himalayan salt
- 1/2 teaspoon pepper
- 1/2 cup spinach, chopped
- 1/4 cup almond flour
- 2 cloves garlic
- 2 tablespoon Italian seasoning
- 8 ounces diced tomatoes

For the ketchup:
- 1 can (8 ounces) tomato sauce
- 1 teaspoon Italian seasoning
- 1/2 teaspoon vinegar

Directions:
1. In a large-sized bowl, mix all of the ingredients except for the potatoes. Shape the meat

mixture into a loaf and then put into the slow cooker. Put the potatoes around the meatloaf.

2. Close the lid of the cooker and cook for 4-6 hours on LOW or for 2-3 hours on HIGH.
3. About 10 minutes before the cooking time is complete, mix the ketchup ingredients until well combined and spread on top of the meatloaf.
4. Close the lid of the cooker and continue cooking for the remaining 10 minutes.
5. Serve the meatloaf and potatoes with asparagus on the side.

Paleo Thai Beef Curry

Prep Time: 10 minutes; **Cook Time:** 4 hours on HIGH

Serving Size: 360 g; **Serves:** 4; **Calories:** 518

Total Fat: 31.7 g **Saturated Fat:** 23.9 g; **Trans Fat:** 0 g

Protein: 42.4 g; **Total Carbs:** 18.4 g

Dietary Fiber: 4.9 g; **Sugars:** 9 g

Cholesterol: 112 mg; **Sodium:** 112 mg; **Potassium:** 1128 mg

Vitamin A: 24%; **Vitamin C:** 160%; **Calcium:** 3%; **Iron:** 151%

Good points: Low in sodium, very high in iron, high in selenium, very high in vitamin B6, very high in vitamin B12, very high in vitamin C, and high in zinc.

Ingredients:
- 500 grams beef steak, diced
- 100 grams mushrooms
- 1 sweet potato
- 1 red pepper
- 1 onion
- 1 green pepper
- 1 can coconut milk
- Cilantro
- Olive oil
- Parsley
- Salt and pepper
- Thai curry paste – about 1 teaspoon

Directions:
1. Preheat the slow cooker for 15 minutes on HIGH setting.
2. In a frying pan, add the olive oil and steak. Cook the steak for about 5 minutes or until browned to seal the juices. Roughly chop the vegetables – be sure to take out the seeds of the

peppers. Put all of the ingredients into the slow cooker and mix until well combined.

3. Add Thai curry paste to suit your taste – the more you put, the spicier the curry will become.
4. Close the lid of the cooker and cook for 4 hours on HIGH. When the cooking time is done, stir to mix everything and season to taste. Serve. This dish is great with Thai cauliflower rice.

Lemon Chicken

Prep Time: 10 minutes; **Cook Time:** 3-4 hours on HIGH	
Serving Size: 277 g; **Serves**: 6-8; **Calories**: 364	
Total Fat: 7.1 g **Saturated Fat**: 2 g; **Trans Fat**: 0 g	
Protein: 66.5 g; **Total Carbs**: 5.6 g	
Dietary Fiber: 1.6 g; **Sugars**: 1.8 g	
Cholesterol: 175 mg; **Sodium**: 533 mg; **Potassium**: 513 mg	
Vitamin A: 5%; **Vitamin C**: 29%; **Calcium**: 5%; **Iron**: 14%	
Good points: Dairy-free, gluten-free, whole30, low in sugar, very high in niacin, high in phosphorus, very high in selenium, and high in vitamin B6.	

Ingredients:
- 1 piece (3-4 pounds) chicken
- 1 onion, quartered
- 1 tablespoon fresh rosemary, minced, plus a few sprigs
- 1 teaspoon garlic powder
- 1 teaspoon onion powder
- 1 teaspoon paprika
- 1 teaspoon salt
- 3 lemons, quartered
- Olive oil

Directions:
1. Put 1/2 of the onion into the bottom of the slow cooker. Put the other 1/2 of the onion and 1 lemon into the cavity of the chicken. Put the chicken on top of the onion in the cooker. Scatter the remaining lemon quarters, and couple sprigs of rosemary around the chicken.
2. In a small-sized bowl, whisk the garlic powder, minced rosemary, paprika, onion powder, and

salt. Drizzle a small amount of olive oil over the top of the chicken and sprinkle the spice blend over the top of the chicken.
3. Close the lid of the cooker and cook for 3-4 hours on HIGH or until the meat is fall-off-the-bone tender.

Slow Cooked Paleo Pot Roast

Prep Time: 20 minutes; **Cook Time:** 10-12 hours on LOW	
Serving Size: 521 g; **Serves:** 6; **Calories:** 699	
Total Fat: 26.6 g **Saturated Fat:** 12.9 g; **Trans Fat:** 0 g	
Protein: 78.9 g; **Total Carbs:** 33.1 g	
Dietary Fiber: 8.7 g; **Sugars:** 10.1 g	
Cholesterol: 229 mg; **Sodium**: 445 mg; **Potassium**: 1439 mg	
Vitamin A: 123%; **Vitamin C**: 49%; **Calcium**: 10%; **Iron**: 55%	
Good points: High in phosphorus, high in selenium, high in vitamin A, high in vitamin B12, and high in zinc.	

Ingredients:
- 3 pounds chuck roast
- 2 pounds parsnips, chopped
- 2 cups carrots, chopped
- 2 cups beef broth
- 2 cloves garlic, chopped
- 1 onion, sliced
- 3 tablespoons coconut oil

Directions:
1. Grease the inside of the slow cooker with the coconut oil.
2. Put coconut oil in a large-sized skillet. Season the roast with pepper and salt. Add to the skillet and cook the roast in the skillet until both sides are seared and well browned.
3. Put the veggies in the bottom of the slow cooker. Put the browned roast on top of the vegetables. Pour the stock over the roast and the veggies.
4. Close the lid of the cooker and cook for 10-12 hours on LOW or until the roast is tender.

5-Ingredient Whole Chicken Paleo Pot

Prep Time: 5 minutes; **Cook Time:** 6-7 hours on LOW; 3-3 1/2 hours on HIGH

Serving Size: 572 g; **Serves**: 4; **Calories:** 847

Total Fat: 27.5 g **Saturated Fat**: 7.8 g; **Trans Fat**: 0 g

Protein: 101.1 g; **Total Carbs:** 43.2 g

Dietary Fiber: 7.4 g; **Sugars:** 6.5 g

Cholesterol: 308 mg; **Sodium**: 382 mg; **Potassium**: 2116 mg

Vitamin A: 386%; **Vitamin C**: 43%; **Calcium**: 11%; **Iron**: 28%

Good points: Low in sodium, low in sugar, high in niacin, high in selenium, very high in vitamin A, and high in vitamin B6.

Ingredients:
- 3-4 pounds whole chicken
- 1 pound carrots, peeled
- 1 pound sweet potatoes, peeled and diced
- 1 tablespoon of your favorite seasoning
- 1 teaspoon ghee

Directions:
1. Rub the seasoning all over the chicken.
2. Add the carrots and potatoes into the slow cooker. Put the chicken on top of the veggies.
3. Add the ghee on top of the chicken.
4. Close the lid of the cooker and cook for 6-7 hours on LOW or for 3-3 1/2 hours on HIGH. Serve.

Paleo Meatballs and Spaghetti Squash

Prep Time: 0 minutes; **Cook Time:** 0 hours	
Serving Size: 569 g; **Serves:** 4-6; **Calories:** 593	
Total Fat: 42.1 g **Saturated Fat:** 11.9 g; **Trans Fat:** 0 g	
Protein: 26.1 g; **Total Carbs:** 32.2 g	
Dietary Fiber: 2.4 g; **Sugars:** 4.5 g	
Cholesterol: 97 mg; **Sodium**: 1430 mg; **Potassium**: 1083 mg	
Vitamin A: 11%; **Vitamin C**: 27%; **Calcium**: 13%; **Iron**: 26%	
Good points: Low in sugar.	

Ingredients:
- 1 spaghetti squash, sized
- 1 pound ground Italian sausage
- 1 can (14 ounces) tomato sauce
- 2 tablespoons hot pepper relish, optional
- 2 tablespoons olive oil
- 4-6 cloves garlic, whole
- Italian seasoning (oregano, thyme, basil) to taste (I used about 2 teaspoons)

Directions:
1. Put the tomato sauce, Italian seasoning, hot pepper relish, garlic, and olive oil into a 6-quart slow cooker.
2. Cut the spaghetti squash crosswise into halve and scoop the seeds out. With the cut side faced down, put the squash in the cooker.
3. Roll the ground sausage into meatballs and fit as many as you can in the sauce around the squash – you can fit about 1/2 a pound worth.
4. Close the lid of the cooker and cook for 5 hours on LOW or for 3 hours on HIGH.

5. When the cooking time is up, remove the squash from the cooker, and using a large fork, pull the spaghetti squash strand. Top the spaghetti squash with the meatballs and pour with the sauce.

Notes: Be sure to use a 6-quart slow cooker for this dish.

Conclusion

Thank you again for purchasing this book. I hope you enjoyed reading it as much as I enjoyed writing it for you!

Finally, if you enjoyed this book, I'd like to ask you to leave a review for my book on Amazon. It would be greatly appreciated!

All the best and good luck,

Andrew Westbrook

Made in the USA
Middletown, DE
29 January 2017